LITERARY LEARNING

Scholarship of Teaching and Learning

Jennifer Meta Robinson

Whitney M. Schlegel

Mary Taylor Huber

Pat Hutchings

editors

LITERARY LEARNING

TEACHING THE ENGLISH MAJOR

SHERRY LEE LINKON

Indiana University Press
Bloomington and Indianapolis

This book is a publication of

Indiana University Press
601 North Morton Street
Bloomington, Indiana 47404-3797 USA

iupress.indiana.edu

Telephone orders   800-842-6796
Fax orders   812-855-7931
Orders by e-mail   iuporder@indiana.edu

Library of Congress Cataloging-in-Publication Data

Linkon, Sherry Lee, [date]
    Literary learning : teaching the English major / Sherry Lee Linkon.
       p.   cm. — (Scholarship of teaching and learning)
    Includes bibliographical references and index.
    ISBN 978-0-253-35699-4 (cloth : alk. paper) — ISBN 978-0-253-22356-2 (pbk. : alk. paper) — ISBN 978-0-253-00559-5 (ebk.)
    1. English literature—Study and teaching (Higher) 2. American literature—Study and teaching (Higher) 3. Literature—Study and teaching (Higher) I. Title.
    PR33.L55   2011
    820.71'1—dc22

                                        2011013252

        1 2 3 4 5   16 15 14 13 12 11

For the people who have taught me the most:
my students and my colleagues

CONTENTS

Preface   ix

1 ▦ The Literary Mind   1

2 ▦ Making Literary Thinking Visible   34

3 ▦ Course Design for Literary Learning   70

4 ▦ Analyzing Students' Learning   105

Appendixes   145

Notes   153

Bibliography   155

Index   159

PREFACE

On a blustery Thursday evening in January, the students in my graduate Working-Class Literature course have gathered around a conference room table. We have a novel and a critical article at hand along with some pretzels and M&Ms to sustain us through our three-hour conversation. The discussion moves quickly and widely between the ideas laid out by the critic and the example of the novel. A question about the writing style in Pietro Di Donato's *Christ in Concrete* evolves into a review of the various ways the novel uses religious references and from there into the relationship between religion, ethnicity, and class, and onward to issues of how readers from different backgrounds might respond. Moving this conversation forward feels effortless, except that I occasionally have to bring one line of thought to a close in order to allow us time to apply another key idea from the critical article to the novel. We laugh often, even though the novel tells a grim story. We're enjoying ourselves, but we're also uncovering serious issues in this novel, considering it as a case that might help us define the broader genre that lies at the heart of the course, and identifying connections with students' personal experiences and academic backgrounds.

This is why I became an English professor, for the pure pleasure of this kind of engaged, critical conversation. I decided to go to graduate school because I thought I'd enjoy teaching, and I had a vague idea that teaching could matter. I believed that the most important outcome of my undergraduate education was the ability to think critically and write well, and I wanted to help others learn these skills. I also found the rhythms of academic life immensely appealing—the flexibility of the daily schedule, the varied work, the balance between interaction with others and solitary, reflective work. I had rejected the idea of becoming a rabbi a few years earlier because I couldn't stand the idea of having to go to school for five more years. But when it came time to graduate, I discovered that I wanted to spend the rest of my life in school.

I didn't know then that becoming a professor would also give me the opportunity to keep learning, not only through my research but also through conversations with students and colleagues. I didn't know that talking about literature could be this much fun or that I would come to believe that it mattered so much. Having this eclectic and critical discussion about this classic working-class novel with these students—who come from working-class families and, in many cases, teach working-class students in a community with a rich and complex working-class history—makes a difference. Like most literature professors, I believe that studying literature helps students learn to understand themselves and the world around them. They learn to read more critically—not just literature but the media, social structures, their own experiences. Every day I appreciate the incredible privilege of having this kind of conversation at the center of my life's work.

From the day I first entered a classroom as a graduate assistant, teaching a first-year composition course, I felt that teaching was my vocation. I enjoy performing, getting a laugh or a nod of recognition from students. Even more, though, I enjoy listening carefully to what they have to say and teasing out how their comments fit with larger ideas or contrast with other people's readings. I'm fascinated with the process of learning, so I'm always curious about students' experiences and how I can help them learn better. For me, teaching is the most consistently engaging activity I do, on personal, political, and intellectual levels.

Because teaching was what I loved most about my work as a professor, I made it a focus of my research from the beginning. At first, because I was teaching women's studies, I explored feminist pedagogies. But since most of my students are first-generation college students and I teach at an open-enrollment state university, I turned my attention to strategies for helping working-class students succeed. In both cases, I explored the intersections between students' personal histories, cultural identities, social positions, and learning experiences. Issues of power, cultural capital, and relationships lay at the heart of that work. Much of my writing at that point aimed at describing effective teaching strategies, with some reference to cultural theories that suggested why they worked.

Yet I also began to be troubled about strategies that didn't work. Why did a carefully designed course not generate the kind of learning I had expected? Why couldn't students perform on their own the kinds of analyses we developed together in class? *Literary Learning* reflects my efforts to discover how to teach better by looking more closely at how students learn. The ideas and strategies presented here reflect a fundamental shift in how I think about teaching students to read and analyze literature better: a shift toward making knowledge and critical practices visible and useable. That shift is a result of a decade of work in the scholarship of teaching and learning. Through conversations and research collaborations with colleagues on my own campus and across the U.S., I've been exposed to theories about learning, acquired new methods for analyzing students' learning more systematically, and developed a clearer sense of what students need to learn, a deeper understanding of the difficulties they encounter, and an array of strategies that facilitate learning. The models laid out in this book reflect insights gained from ten years of individual research and significant conversations with colleagues.

Near the end of those ten years, my department began revising the English major and developing a plan for assessing students' learning. To begin the process, the assessment committee talked with each member of the department, asking everyone what they thought an English major should know. We then drafted a fairly lengthy set of "learning outcomes," statements that attempted to synthesize our long and varied lists of possible goals. We said that students should develop tools for close reading, including the ability to use literary terms. They should understand various theories and strategies for studying literature. They should understand the "dominant genres, central themes, and major figures of literary movements from the medieval period through the present."

Even though I had pushed for and remained a believer in the value of defining goals, I found our lists strangely unsatisfying. I didn't disagree with any of them. They simply didn't capture the complexity of what we meant. Of course, it is the nature of goal statements, especially goals for a whole major, to represent large, diverse bodies of knowledge and ways of knowing. Our goals were necessarily framed in broad ways, allowing plenty of space for interpretation and individual preferences. Perhaps we were simply avoiding conflict, but quick agreement meant that we spent little time articulating our ideas. We approved learning outcomes without much discussion, and so they provided little substantive guidance about what and how we should teach or what we should expect students to learn. What did we mean when we said that students should understand "what literary criticism is and how it can contribute to interpretation"? What did they need to learn in order to not only understand that concept but also put it into practice? We all agreed on the goal, but could that statement in itself help us figure out how to teach about literary criticism?

For me, the answer was plainly no. Understanding the nature and uses of literary criticism, like all of our goals, represents a complex set of concepts, information, and strategies. For example, in order to achieve an understanding of the nature and uses of literary criticism, students would have to recognize that reading is always a critical act, that it is always enacted through theory, though our theories don't always fit into the neatly labeled categories commonly presented in undergraduate theory courses. They would have to understand the difference between reading and interpreting, and they would have to believe that interpretation serves a purpose. Students would have to see themselves as joining a circle of informed and engaged critical readers that includes other students and the professor as well as literary critics, other writers, and everyday readers. They would need to understand that interpretations are not right or wrong but better or worse, persuasive or not. Students would need to understand that the discourse community they are joining has a well-developed set of conventions and standards, as well as a shared body of knowledge, which means that they would have to understand at least some of those conventions, standards, and knowledge as well as the concept of a discourse community.

I enjoy this kind of unpacking and find it useful, and I like to think that many of my colleagues would also have enjoyed such a discussion, but we didn't have that kind of conversation about our goals. On several occasions as we worked on the new major, someone would comment, "We should really have a serious conversation about what we think English majors should learn." We never did. Few departments in any discipline ever do. Such discussions take a lot of time, and we wanted to complete our new major plan within a year, so that we could move into implementation. But who ever has time for that kind of long, reflective conversation? Such discussions can also raise concerns about losing our freedom to teach what and how we like (because each of us is sure that our way works best). But even that doesn't explain our aversion to critical discussion of what it means to learn about literature. Rather, the problem is that we are all experts in the same field, so we take for granted the complex meanings of the terms and nuances of literary knowledge. The core ideas of our shared discipline are so implicit, so already understood, that they don't seem to require definition. Why take valuable time to discuss something as obvious as what it means to understand literary history?

In other words, our resistance to exploring the goals makes perfect sense. But not talking about them ensured that they were essentially useless, because they stated obvious generalities instead of describing our shared analysis of what literary understanding involves. Not surprisingly, as we moved through the process of planning the major, the goals were hardly mentioned. We made few decisions that overtly violated them, but our decisions were also not guided by them in any meaningful way. Of course, we argued about some aspects of the curriculum, but most of those debates had to do with coverage or the balance between literature and writing. Should all of our students take a course on Shakespeare? Should our "major figures" course always look at Milton, Spenser, or Joyce, or could it examine any significant writer? Should an English major take advanced writing courses, or only courses in literature and language? Almost no one used the goals to support an argument in these debates.

The process of revising the major left me curious about the nature and content of literary knowledge. What values, knowledge, and thinking practices lay behind my colleagues' almost universal agreement that students needed better "coverage" of literary history? What did they mean when they said that students needed to "understand and be able to deploy literary terminology"? What did these concepts mean to me? While I knew that articulating what students should learn in the English major would not be easy, and I understood why my department and probably most literature faculty resist taking the time to do so, I was also convinced that such analysis could help us teach better. While I already had some ideas about how students learn to read and write well about literature, my department's conversations about the structure and content of the English major made me want to learn more about how literary scholars think.

Through research on my own students' learning, reading research from within literary studies and composition, and exploring ideas about learning from other fields, I've reached four conclusions that shape this book:

- One of the keys to teaching better is understanding more fully the nature of our own knowledge; the more conscious we are of how our own minds work, the more effectively we can help students develop similar habits of mind.

- We can help students acquire literary habits of mind by making our ways of thinking, our strategic knowledge, more visible in the classroom; when strategic thinking emerges from between the lines, it becomes easier for students to recognize and use.

- Learning how to think about literature is a process, and we should guide and coach students through that process; we can achieve that by designing courses and assignments that clearly emphasize both content and strategic knowledge, that give students opportunities to practice applying this knowledge, and that offer formative advice as they practice.

- We can improve our teaching by studying our students' learning; when faculty ask critical questions, as individuals and as departments, about why students struggle and what helps them succeed, we can improve their learning and make our own teaching lives more enjoyable.

This book is organized around those four ideas. It begins with a discussion of literary expertise. What do we know that allows us to read and analyze literature well? It then explores strategies for making literary ways of thinking more visible in the classroom. What would it mean to pay more attention to strategic knowledge, to give it a more central place in our pedagogy? That discussion focuses on the level of the class session or a series of a few sessions. But teaching and learning occur over the course of a semester. How can we develop students' abilities over time? How can we structure courses, assignments, and classroom experiences sequentially and incrementally to build students' abilities and confidence? *Literary Learning* ends with a discussion of how we can learn from our students and find solutions to the teaching problems that we all face. If we want to teach well, we should look critically at students' responses to our teaching strategies to identify what does and does not work, what students need, and what literary learning means.

Literary Learning reflects the guidance and collaboration of many colleagues and the support of several institutions. My intellectual guides through this journey, Randy Bass, Mary Huber, and Pat Hutchings, have introduced me to key ideas, talked through my research as well as the manuscript for this book, and directed me to other colleagues who provided crucial assistance. Their wisdom and enthusiasm have carried me through a decade of exploration. Under their auspices, I participated in two programs that shaped much of my research: the Carnegie Scholars program and the Visible Knowledge Project. Youngstown State University provided support for my participation in these programs and provided a research leave to allow me to complete this book. The Center for New Designs in Learning and Scholarship at Georgetown University invited me to be a scholar-in-residence for two periods, during which many of the ideas in this book took shape. At Georgetown, I was guided by Susannah McGowan, Michael Coventry, and John Rakestraw, insightful colleagues who generously set aside their own work to talk about mine. The Carnegie Foundation for the Advancement of Teaching provided an incredibly beautiful workspace and the quiet necessary for substantive writing. Several colleagues at Youngstown State, including Corey Andrews, Suzanne Diamond, Tim Francisco, Pat Hauschildt, Martha Pallante, Melissa Smith, and Stephanie Tingley, have talked with me about their teaching and my research. I have come to rely upon Michael Coventry and Linda Adler-Kassner as critical readers, friends I can count on to tell me when I'm off track. Mariolina Salvatori provided both wise advice as well as a model for how to write about students' learning in literature courses. Students in my English and American studies courses over the years have not only tolerated my experiments but also generously shared their work and their reflections on their learning experiences. I am grateful for all of the advice, support, criticism, and comradeship that made this work possible. Finally, my family contributed more personally to this project. My sister, Carey Pickus, and her family, with assistance from our parents, Helene and Gordon Linkon, provided shelter and productive distractions while I worked at Carnegie. My husband, John Russo, my partner-in-all-things, understood that I needed to do this on my own; his daily love makes possible everything I do.

LITERARY LEARNING

1 ▪ The Literary Mind

Most of us become English professors because we love reading and talking about what we read. The pleasures of the text lie not only in the private experience of silent reading but in the interactive experience of comparing notes. Yet teaching literature, like all teaching, has its frustrations. We've all encountered resistance from students who dislike the texts we love. Students sometimes read poorly, missing nuances of meaning or aesthetic qualities. They may have difficulty moving from personal response—I liked it, I had a similar experience—to interpretation. They may struggle to construct appropriate arguments, or they may raise questions that seem completely irrelevant. They miss irony and satire, ignore form, and acknowledge style in only the most general of terms. Faculty explain these student difficulties in several ways. Students just don't read, we complain, or they don't read the right stuff. They have grown up in a multimedia culture that doesn't value literature. They're not willing to work at it.

Theorizing about what's wrong with our students may have its satisfactions. But, as educational psychologist Sam Wineburg suggests, the truth may be more troubling than our hypotheses. In writing about the "habits of mind" that distinguish expert historians from the best history students, Wineburg argues that students' difficulties in reading may not stem from their weaknesses. The problem, he writes, may be simply that "no one has ever bothered to teach them some basic but powerful skills of interpretation." The answer, he proposes, is for us to make our ways of thinking more visible, "to show our students the patient and painstaking processes" of scholarly thinking. Wineburg concludes,

"Only by making our footsteps visible can we expect students to follow in them" (2003). His analysis reflects one of the major conclusions of the past few decades of research on learning: understanding involves not only knowing the material but also learning how to think. For college students in any major, that means learning the key content of the field as well as acquiring disciplinary habits of mind.

If we want to help students develop literary minds, we must begin by considering the nature of literary knowledge—not only knowledge about literature but also ways of thinking about texts and language. We want students to learn how to think well about literature and language not because we expect them all to become great literary scholars; few will ultimately pursue that path. So while English programs foreground literary history and theory, we also proclaim the value of the critical thinking and communication skills that students acquire along the way. We recognize the value of literary habits of mind—what I call *strategic knowledge*—but we rarely talk about what it involves. Nor do we always make its presence clear in the design of the major or even in individual courses. Strategic knowledge is always present in literary studies, but it isn't always visible.

Content Knowledge and Strategic Knowledge

The content of literary studies seems obvious, even though the boundaries of the field are not precisely defined: we study major texts, movements, and genres; the core ideas of various schools of literary theory; and some basic tools and terms for literary analysis, such as form, style, research tools, and conventions for documenting and citing sources. With significant variations depending on specialties and experience, all literary scholars know this material. In various forms, this content appears in the anthologies, textbooks, and handbooks used in literature courses. In most English departments, the curriculum is organized around these topics, most often with an emphasis on literary history. Commonly, the major begins with surveys that introduce the history of literature, and students then take upper-level courses that examine particular periods, writers, genres, or theories in some depth. Some programs include courses on linguistics, writing, and other media, and some include an introductory course about how to read and write in the discipline. While a few departments use other approaches, this model remains fairly standard.

While our discipline is defined by its content, research on learning suggests that content knowledge becomes functional through the application of strategic knowledge: habits of mind, assumptions, attitudes, and critical practices. A literary reader must not only know the relevant content, such as how a text fits in literary history or the term to describe a particular style feature; s/he must also be able to apply knowledge about literary history and terminology to identify and explore significant aspects of the text and to explain them effectively. Without content knowledge, strategy is useless. Without strategy, content knowledge is quickly forgotten.

No doubt, as John V. Knapp notes in a survey of scholarship on student learning and the teaching of literature, we have come a long way from the days when teaching literature meant lecturing about content (51). Traditional ways of teaching fit well with the goals of New Criticism, focusing students' attention on a well-defined and supposedly teachable method of literary analysis. This approach also reinforced the idea that only the expert, the teacher, had the "right" reading. By the 1970s, reader-response theory began to influence college teaching, as faculty began to use in the classroom the ideas first put forward by Louise Rosenblatt in her 1938 *Literature as Exploration*. David Bleich extended this approach by connecting reader response with psychology in his *Subjective Criticism*.[1] During the same era, discussions of feminist and critical pedagogies encouraged faculty across the disciplines to emphasize "student-centered teaching," which was sometimes inspired by ideals of egalitarian classrooms or by Freirean arguments about education as empowerment. In the late '80s and early '90s, the rise of feminist theory, multiculturalism, and the new historicism fostered a wave of books, mostly essay collections, exploring how new insights about the politics of the classroom should reshape the teaching of literature.[2] Many of these discussions emphasized strategies for more actively engaging students by giving them more responsibility for selecting texts, directing discussions, or teaching each other, while others focused on content—expanding the canon, devising strategies for helping white and middle-class students interact productively with texts by working-class writers and by people of color, incorporating theory into the classroom. Jane Tompkins's 1990 essay, "Pedagogy of the Distressed," which outlined a strategy that put students in charge of planning and leading discussions, sparked many conversations in English departments about how to engage students more actively, but by the time her memoir, *A Life in School,* appeared in 1997, those ideas were no longer so new or radical. Books such as these, together with journals such as *Pedagogy* and *College English* and the long-standing MLA Approaches to Teaching series, make clear that as a discipline we have a continuing interest in pedagogy, and our teaching methods are evolving in ways that reflect theoretical and political perspectives.

Yet even as our discipline has embraced more interactive classroom modes, we have not explored the findings of scholars in education and psychology who have been analyzing how people learn and what teaching strategies best facilitate learning. Writing in 1990, Janet Emig noted that college-level literature teachers had ignored theories about teaching and learning for too long. She warned that if college-level English faculty did not begin to pay attention to these theories, the field would "continue to lose its constituency, the possible future English major, and continue to fail the general student population, thus contributing ironically—that is, unintentionally, but formidably—to the literacy crisis in higher education" (88). Like Emig, Knapp suggests that if we look beyond our disciplinary borders, we will find much in studies of expertise that is "both useful and philosophically compatible with good humanistic teaching practices" (53). Knapp provides a useful overview, as does John Bransford et al.'s *How People Learn: Brain, Mind, Experience, and School,* a 1999 report that synthesized scientific research on learning and suggested applications for classrooms. These sources provide valuable insight into the difficulties students encounter in learning to think well about literature and how we can help them overcome those challenges.

How People Learn begins with a discussion of "how experts differ from novices." While some find the terminology of "experts" and "novices" off-putting, the core concept goes far to help us understand the challenges involved in helping students develop literary knowledge. Experts notice significant patterns and features that novices simply don't see. This happens in part because experts' content knowledge is at once extensive and, crucially, organized into categories and relationships that reflect disciplinary ideas and facilitate quick retrieval of appropriate knowledge for a given situation. Experts don't just know "the facts"; they also know how the facts relate to each other and the broad concepts that give meaning to those facts. Among experts in any given field, individuals will know some aspects of the field better than others, but at best, experts have what Bransford et al. call "adaptive expertise," the ability to adjust and change our ways of thinking to fit new situations. Experts adapt by using both disciplinary knowledge and "metacognitive skills," the ability to evaluate their own thinking, identify difficulties, and select alternative strategies.[3] We use our knowledge and ability comfortably, almost without deliberate effort or intention. For most English professors, literary thinking feels natural, almost obvious.

Consider the experience of responding to a student's question in class. We can usually respond substantively (if perhaps not perfectly) by offering an explanation of a concept, a theoretical perspective, a term, or an example, and we do so with relative ease. We don't have to mentally survey everything we know; instead, we focus immediately on the relevant elements of an extensive body of knowledge. In our literary research, we make similar seemingly intuitive moves, shifting among topics, sources, and approaches to the text or problem we're exploring, again because our knowledge of the literature itself, its historical context, relevant theory, and the practice of literary research is embedded in webs of related information. We can do that because our knowledge is organized into clusters that reflect the core assumptions and practices of our field. This well-structured knowledge gives us fluency.

Imagine how difficult it would be if you had to begin every research project by sorting through everything you know about literary studies in order to determine where to begin. Imagine if you had to do this in the middle of class in order to respond to a student's question. If we didn't know literary texts, the history of literature, theoretical perspectives, and concepts well, if that knowledge were not organized efficiently, and if we couldn't use it effectively, we couldn't do our jobs. For us, using literary knowledge well comes easily, but our students are in the early stages of building a well-structured body of content and strategic knowledge. If they struggle to find a smart way to approach a research project or to respond to an exam question, the problem may not be a lack of understanding of the specific material but simply that they don't yet have enough experience with literary thinking. As experts, we see useful pathways into literary problems clearly, often without conscious effort, and our students' struggles can be puzzling.

This, Bransford and his colleagues explain, is why expertise can hinder good teaching (32–33). Experts forget what it's like to not understand concepts that they find extremely simple and clear. Aspects of texts that are obvious to us as experts are often invisible to our students, because they don't yet have a well-structured body of content knowledge, and they have not yet acquired the disciplinary habits of mind to make appropriate use of what they do know. Students' difficulties are not necessarily evidence of their lack of ability or effort. Rather, their struggles reflect the process of learning. One of my colleagues, a professor of Russian, suggests that we think of ourselves as "native speakers" of the "language" of literary studies, while our students are acquiring a second language.[4] As majors, our literature students may have mastered the basics, but they are far from fluent. Native speakers of a language don't have to think about how to put together a reasonable sentence or whether to put the adjective before or after the noun. Such things come naturally. Indeed, most native speakers cannot explain the logic of the grammar they use (mostly) correctly every day. The same may be said of the way literary scholars notice, identify, and describe the differences between types of novels or literary movements. For us, such understanding seems natural and obvious. But it's unfair for us to expect our students to think like experts; our job is to help them learn to function in the discipline, much as a good student of German can converse but not yet, perhaps, dream in her second language.

The strategic knowledge that gives us fluency in our discipline is harder to define than content knowledge, because our use of it is largely unconscious. Strategic knowledge functions much like what Pierre Bourdieu terms "habitus," the habits of mind grounded in a specific culture and situation that guide human behavior. Writing about the habitus of sociology, Bourdieu suggests that it operates "as a matrix of perceptions, appreciations, and actions" (qtd. in Brubaker 213). Scholars rely on these habitual ways of thinking in a wide variety of research and teaching tasks; the habitus "can engender an infinite variety of practices." Sociologist Rogers Brubaker suggests: "It is the habitus that determines the kinds of problems that are posed, the kinds of explanations that are offered, and the kinds of instruments (conceptual, methodological, statistical) that are employed. More important, the habitus determines the *manner* in which problems are posed, explanations constructed, and instruments employed" (213). The habitus regulates the practice of a discipline "in an unconscious, unintentional manner; it is a 'modus operandi that is not consciously mastered,' a 'spontaneity with neither consciousness nor will.'" Brubaker also suggests that these internalized "rules" are especially important in fields where methods and standards of proof are not "rationalized" and "codified" (214), such as literary studies. As Bransford and his colleagues suggest about expertise, Brubaker notes that "practical mastery may even be incompatible with conscious symbolic mastery; self-consciousness can inhibit or even destroy the practical efficacy of the habitus" (225). These internalized strategies and attitudes shape our conscious thinking, and competence requires that we not have to think about how we think.

The literary habitus does not take the form of a well-articulated set of rules. Some disciplines have clearly defined methods and standards of proof, but whatever consensus exists in literary studies reflects shared values and attitudes rather than explicit methodology. Our discipline defines itself, in part, by its broad scope, diverse theoretical and methodological approaches, ever-expanding body of texts, and ongoing debates. Some have suggested that the field is becoming more fragmented over time, as scholars specialize ever more narrowly. Reflecting on fifty years in the discipline, J. Hillis Miller notes, "What used to make sense as a rational discipline, with identifiable rules and goals, no longer does, at least in many departments," though he goes on to acknowledge that visions of a previously unified discipline are "slightly exaggerated" (64). Perhaps because literary studies engages such varied approaches, "literary understandings cannot," Susan Hynds writes, "be developed discretely as a set of skills" (122). Northrop Frye's 1957 claim that "the mental process involved" in studying literature "is as coherent and progressive as the study of science" may seem wrongheaded today, but we might agree with his suggestion that literary learning involves "a precisely similar training of the mind" (10–11).

While our disciplinary practice is neither unified nor codified, and we may debate endlessly the various ways of interpreting and explaining literature, we do have a common disciplinary culture, one that reflects the history of literary theory and critical practice. For all our diversity, we share some basic attitudes, habits, and assumptions. These literary ways of thinking are at once central in our teaching and often unnamed. We use them in the classroom every day, and we expect English majors to develop them, but we rarely make them the overt object of pedagogical attention. Doing so can, I believe, facilitate students' learning, as I will discuss in subsequent chapters, but before we can consider how to teach literary thinking, we must identify its elements.

Elements of Literary Thinking

Describing the strategic knowledge of literary studies seems, at first, like an exercise in stating the obvious. The habits of mind that allow us to read and analyze literature well may seem like common sense. But research on expertise suggests that cognitive habits that appear to come "naturally" are actually acquired abilities, special ways of thinking that our students do not yet have and must develop. As Wineburg argues, we can facilitate student learning by making these habits visible, but we cannot do that unless we are conscious of them ourselves. What follows is my attempt to map three key aspects of literary strategic knowledge: dispositions, ways of reading, and protocols for literary argument. Just as content categories like literary history and literary genres overlap, these categories are interwoven. Our dispositions shape how we read, and our argumentative practices reflect both. In addition, as the discussion below will make clear, strategic knowledge is developed and facilitated through content knowledge, and vice versa.

Dispositions

Everything we do in teaching and studying literature is rooted in our dispositions, the attitudes and values that lie at the heart of the discipline. For all of the arguments that divide literary scholars, we share some basic assumptions, beginning with the belief that literature matters. As Elaine Showalter writes, "all of us who teach literature believe that it is important not only in education but in life" (24). Introductory notes and statements of purpose from English department websites around the country offer variations on this theme. The Indiana University website begins with this claim: "The study of language and literature is really the study of life. The stories we find in literature, and the language used to tell such stories, connects us in myriad ways to much larger worlds, both past and present." This idea of the value of literature is part of what attracts some students to the field. As one student explained, "Literature gives most people, myself included, a different perspective on life. It influences your life, influences you to do something with your life, influences your thinking, your ways of dealing with people in general."[5] We study literature not solely for its beauty or even to understand its aesthetic principles, but because it provides the opportunity to see the world through someone else's eyes and, in the process, understand ourselves better. The complexity and nuance of literary language, together with the narratives and perspectives offered by literature, help us understand how to "read" the world around us and help us understand our own experiences and motivations. This is, on one level, a thoroughly humanist, even universalist assumption. As a discipline, we have, at times, been almost embarrassed by this belief. It can seem sappy, naïve, idealistic.

In earlier periods, and in some circles today, literary scholars have attempted to counter this highly subjective, personal way of thinking about literature with models that promise objectivity and concrete methodology. But, as Bleich might remind us, such attempts cannot erase the emotional and intellectual pleasure of losing oneself in an especially moving text. After all, what in the world matters more than understanding the motivations and consequences of human behavior, the perspectives of others from the past as well as the present, the complex and often contradictory workings of the human brain and heart? As literary studies has changed over time, our ideas about how literature reveals human experience have shifted. Wary of ignoring differences across time, place, and culture, we may no longer so easily claim *Romeo and Juliet* as a "universal love story," but even our most contextualized, political readings are based on the idea that literature can teach us about human experience. That human experience is now seen as specific—a Shakespeare class today might well explore how *Romeo and Juliet* reflects the social tensions of the sixteenth century—but the value of literature to our understanding of each other remains central.

For most contemporary literary scholars, literature is fundamentally cultural. Context matters—for both writers and readers. The creation and the consumption of literature are grounded in time and place. The author has a position—within society and history, but also in relation to the issues, events, characters, and places he or she writes about. Writers cannot help but employ the cultural vocabulary of the moment, even in work that is not overtly political or purposeful. The same applies to readers, both the original readers of a text and the current reader. Thus, literature is influenced and illuminated by its context even as it provides a lens for understanding the context of the text and our own culture. As Michael A. Elliott and Claudia Stokes note in the introduction to a 2003 collection of essays on literary methodology, literary studies today employs "a diverse and varied interpretive toolbox, one organized chiefly around the enduring critical discussion of the relation between the literary text and the culture(s) in which it is composed and, as some critics might venture, read" (4). Not surprisingly, in an online survey of literature faculty from around the country, the most popular answer to the question of what students most need to learn was understanding "ideas about how literature reflects the social issues of its time."[6]

Literary scholars recognize that literature, like human experience, is complex. What appears on the surface is never the whole story, and we take pleasure in the puzzles and challenges of literary texts. Perhaps because of the influence of modernism, postmodernism, and New Criticism, we value texts that experiment with language and form, that offer complex structures and internal tensions—texts that invite *work*. But we wrestle with seemingly simple texts too, because we believe that "reading between the lines" and "against the grain" can reveal qualities and meanings that are not immediately evident. For literary scholars, wrestling and playing with texts are both fun and profitable, so to speak. In general education courses, where most are not majoring in English, students regularly complain about "reading too much into" poems and stories. To them, this critical process appears excessive and redundant. Once they know what a text is about, they're ready to move on. For English majors, though, as for scholars, the whole point of reading is to explore what the text offers and what we can do with it. We choose this field because we love to discuss what we read. As one student put it, "I love talking about the texts and deconstructing them and the biographies of the authors, what their motives were, what their life was like." For literary scholars and most English majors, exploring the complexity of a text is pleasurable and significant.

These first few dispositions are typical not only of English professors but also of many English majors. Students become English majors because they love to read or because they want to become writers, and they share the expert's pleasure in playing with texts and the belief that literature matters. Indeed, these dispositions may well be shared by most people who enjoy reading literature. We might even say that these assumptions and attitudes lead people to become readers. Literary scholars begin with these dispositions, but as we develop expertise, we acquire a few additional habits of mind.

The first, and perhaps most important, is awareness of the text as a construction, not as a "natural" or transparent representation of reality. Although in classroom conversations and even in some scholarly writing we might discuss characters and narrators as if they were real people, we are always aware that this is a posture. Our belief that literature is cultural draws our attention to how it reflects reality, but our view of literature as art leads us not only to be aware of but also to appreciate the text as a construction. Because of this, we are always aware of the presence of the author—an individual with a perspective based on a specific cultural context, social position, and life history, who has imagined a world and a situation, invented characters, crafted a voice, and made hundreds of decisions and probably a number of revisions in constructing the text. The author may not have intended all of the possible effects or responses (and even the best of intentions will not necessarily control how the text works), but he or she nonetheless thought and labored over the text. Thus, we navigate a complex terrain of representation and imagination, intention and effect—a terrain that we find both comfortable and engaging. That combination of the real and the imaginary, what we find and what the author may have intended, gives literature its power as well as its pleasure. It is, together with language itself, what creates the puzzle of a text.

The pleasure we take in wrestling with texts reflects a more general disposition: an appreciation for complexity and ambiguity. Here again, literary studies is fundamentally humanist, in the sense that contemporary literary scholars embrace subjectivity (in all its meanings) and resist claims to objectivity. Literary scholarship integrates personal response and imagination, which are inherently individual and emotional, with analytical and intellectual elements, such as comparison with other texts, response to previous analysis, and engagement with current and sometimes past discourse in the field.

Literary studies embraces a wide range of approaches, theories, and materials. This diversity reflects the field's appreciation for creativity, multiplicity, and complexity. In *Learning to Think,* a study of cognitive strategies and patterns in various disciplines, Janet Gail Donald describes English as "organized around the production of consensual knowledge arrived at through contention rather than the empirical testing of theories as in the sciences" (236). Literary studies, she notes, is among the most "divergent" of disciplines; scholars in the field agree on relatively little compared with other disciplines. This lack of "collective coherence" does not simply provide "commensurate freedom to explore," as Donald puts it (237); divergence is, for literary scholars, a positive value. It is not only that we appreciate having the freedom to explore multiple meanings and approaches. Rather, we believe that multiple approaches yield better readings and that it is the nature of literature to embody multiple, complex, and often contradictory meanings. The complexity and ambiguity of texts make multiple readings both possible and necessary. Indeed, as Donald suggests, the "most useful truth a student can learn" in studying literature "is that a piece of literature yields different insights depending on the questions put to it" (242). While some students find this frustrating, for literature faculty, that openness is an invitation to exploration and play.

Ambiguity is a key word in literary studies. While it has some specific meanings, most famously laid out in William Empson's 1930 volume, *Seven Types of Ambiguity,* in practice today, ambiguity might be better described as a disposition than as a concrete, specific term. It references the qualities of literature that create the opportunity for interpretation—how the myriad ways that we might approach a text can yield different meanings and nuances. But it also reminds us that the practice of literary study is, indeed, about interpreting rather than about determining definitive answers. Literary scholars value the potential for and the practice of generating and debating the multiple interpretations of a text. Nathan A. Scott Jr. notes that the discipline values "that virtue which Keats considered to be essential to any serious literary venture— Negative Capability, the capacity for tolerance of the ambiguous and the problematical" (52). While some of our students and our colleagues in other fields may view the open-endedness of our field as evidence that ours is really not a *discipline,* for us this quality of our work is a strength. It reflects our view that the world itself as well as human interaction and communication are inherently ambiguous.

"Negative Capability"

Our comfort with the open-ended quality of literary discourse is based, in part, on self-confidence. We trust ourselves as readers, so our response to difficulty is often perseverance and even pleasure. Our expertise allows us to enjoy the challenge of a difficult text, because it provides an opportunity to exercise our critical muscles. This confidence rests on what cognitive psychologists call *adaptive expertise,* which is itself a function of metacognition. As Sheridan Blau writes, "Unlike our students, we seem to have a fairly sophisticated capacity to recognize and talk about the condition of our understanding. We know the difference between what we do and don't understand and to what degree we do or don't understand" (41). Experts in any field have the ability to monitor their own thinking, to evaluate how well an approach is working, and to identify alternative strategies, while those who are just learning may not have a clear vision of what they know or how to proceed. Novice readers are more likely to give up, blame the text for being too hard (or the teacher for assigning such a difficult text), or blame themselves for not being smart enough to understand. When I asked students to describe how they would approach analyzing a difficult text, almost none offered an interpretive strategy. Instead, they suggested ways of finding answers from experts. Most indicated that they would read critical articles, and a few suggested that they would look at web pages such as SparkNotes. Others said that they would hope that the text would become clear in class discussion. Alternatively, they told me, they would simply keep rereading the text and hope that clarity would eventually emerge. None could identify a specific critical strategy or approach that would help. As they struggled to make sense of an unfamiliar poem, nearly every student explained the difficulty of the task in terms of his or her individual limitations. The problem was, student after student confided, "I'm just not good with poetry." Literary scholars, in contrast, know that the text itself together with the insights yielded by exploring contextual information, theoretical stances, and sheer perseverance will ultimately lead us to a satisfactory reading. And if our initial efforts fail, that may mean that we have stumbled upon a literary problem, and a research project might emerge. For us, difficulty can be productive.[7]

Ways of Reading

These dispositions shape our interactions with literature, but reading itself is the most significant element of strategic knowledge in literary studies. Literary scholars read well, but what does that mean, and how do we do it? Good reading, the kind of reading that we want our students to learn, resists definition. Scholars and theorists who study reading have struggled to explain what happens when experts read. As with many issues in the humanities, scholars do not agree but rather offer several distinct theories. Kathleen McCormick provides a useful overview of some of the dominant theories, distilling a large body of theoretical work into three models, which she terms *cognitive, expressivist,* and *social-cultural.* Cognitive approaches emphasize the reader's thought process, how he or she makes meaning by engaging in certain definable strategies, including drawing on prior knowledge and fitting new information into an existing "schema" (16–17). Expressivists focus on reader response, noting that readers make meaning subjectively, as their own emotional and intellectual connections affect what they notice and the meaning they create in the text. The social-cultural model emphasizes the social context in which reading occurs and the "cultural resources" that shape readers' interactions with texts (48).

While McCormick takes care to examine the nuances that divide these approaches, she ultimately shows that they are not necessarily antithetical. She offers a cultural studies model that incorporates elements of all three schools of thought. Her approach "regards the reader as actively constructing meaning, not as a free individual, but as a subject in history who nonetheless possesses some degree of agency." Reading, McCormick argues, "is not fully 'determined' by the social situation (which would enable it to be easily predictable), nor is it fully controlled by the reader's subjectivity." Readers construct meaning within the boundaries of their culture and the culture of the text, and, as the cognitive theorists would argue, they draw upon literary and cultural schema as they struggle to make sense of new material. Yet, as McCormick points out, "readers encounter such a wealth of complex and contradictory ideological forces that they must continually negotiate among them" (57–58). Her approach defines reading as an active but not always intentional process.

The idea that reading is a complex process that resists clear description runs through much of the discussion of how both ordinary readers and literary scholars interact with texts. Robert Scholes approaches reading as a craft, a practice that involves a range of specific practices and strategies that work together in complex ways to focus our attention and allow us to develop interpretations. In *Protocols of Reading,* he defines reading as "a creative process in which we generate, use, and discard our own texts as a way of making sense of the text we are ostensibly 'reading'" (1989 8). Scholes shows what he means by offering a reading of a seventeenth-century painting attributed to Georges de La Tour, *The Education of the Virgin,* which depicts a young girl reading by candlelight a book that is held on the lap of a woman. He suggests how we might move from identifying what the painting shows to looking at details of shadow and composition before considering how this work is related to others from the same period and how the title shapes our interpretation of what we see. He raises a question about the image— "What is she reading?"—and considers the painter's setting, among his family, but also the idea that the painting might have been intended as a representation of Mary, and he asks what people in de La Tour's world might have thought that Mary would read. "Let us say," he suggests, that the book is the Bible, offering a tentative, provisional answer to his own question, and he then moves into speculation about what that might signify (1989 4–5). Scholes acknowledges that his example reflects just one version of the process. Another reader might have posed a different question or drawn on different associations and resources as he or she pondered possible answers.

Like McCormick, Scholes suggests that reading is an active, dialectical process that involves paying attention to the details and structure of the text, drawing on contextual knowledge, posing questions, taking provisional positions, and exploring hypotheses: "Reading, it cannot be emphasized too much, takes place in time. It is not just a matter of finding the 'best' metaphor or other figure to understand a complex text, it is a matter of moving through a series of figures that enable us to understand our textual object better" (1989 8). This process is fluid and often unconscious. Reading may involve a variety of strategies, but they are integrated into an activity that we have difficulty describing in any specificity. While some key elements are probably common to most literary scholars—looking at the text on the level of both story and execution, considering the author's context, posing questions, developing hypotheses—in practice, the process of reading is sufficiently individual, complex, and malleable that it cannot be reduced to a formula. We cannot describe the process as a series of steps to be followed, but we can identify some of the qualities and common practices involved in expert reading, the cognitive habits that experts use in reading and analyzing literary texts.

So, how do good readers approach a text? What is involved in expert reading? First, expert reading is attentive to the text itself. While a recent resurgence of debate about close reading suggests that literary critics don't fully agree about how much emphasis to place on the text, careful reading is, and probably always will be, the most basic skill of literary studies. Indeed, as Don Bialostosky suggests in a debate about the place of close reading in literary studies, the term tells us relatively little: "it leaves entirely to the discretion (or to the unexamined predispositions) of 'close' readers what they attend to or what they make of what they attend to" (112). Andrew DuBois, in the introduction to a collection of critical articles reflecting different varieties of close reading by both formalist and more contextual critics, suggests that, however we define it, "paying attention" is what makes for "reading well." This, he claims, "will, over time, with personally productive tendencies or habits of focus and repetitions of thought remembered into generally applicable patterns, beget method" (2). In another volley of the debate, Jane Gallop argues that close reading is "the very thing that made us a discipline" (183). For all the bluster of the recent debate, everyone seems to agree that reading literature involves, as Bialostosky puts it, "productive attentiveness to literary texts" (113).

What habits of mind make for "productive attention"? Perhaps the most important element of good reading, and in some ways the core of close reading, is a facility with and an appreciation for language. Literary scholars have large and varied vocabularies, but they also understand how words and grammar work, know something about the history of language, and recognize both unusual and idiomatic uses of language. Literary scholars appreciate the slippery and indeterminate nature of language. An expert reader knows that a single word or phrase might have multiple meanings or function in multiple ways at once. Moreover, for an expert reader, the tension between the fluid, layered, even conflicted nature of language and the idea that good reading should be "true" to the text is at once pleasurable and productive. As part of my research, I wanted to compare how experienced literary scholars and English majors dealt with an unfamiliar text. I used a research tool called a "think-aloud," in which I asked each individual to read and begin to interpret an unfamiliar poem and to vocalize their thoughts as they did so.[8] While both groups paid attention to the language of the poem, the students moved fairly quickly from noting interesting phrases to formulating a story to identify the speaker and situation. The professors, however, spent more time with the language. They read phrases out loud, repeatedly, often without comment. Voicing the lines seemed sufficient, as if it were itself a form of thinking. The scholars' comments focused on the beauty of the language and on nuances in the words and images. Despite my repeated requests for readers to articulate what they were thinking, the professors' most common response was simply to read and reread the lines. When students and professors did comment on the language, they did so in different ways. Students noted unusual words, but they focused primarily on phrases that confused them, struggling to paraphrase the poem. The professors commented on the sound and texture of the language, and they identified tensions and connections between different phrases and words. The expert readers displayed both appreciation for and a habit of paying attention to language, while most of the students were less attentive to and less engaged by it.

As this example suggests, reading well involves not only understanding how language works, but also the ability to determine easily how to engage with language. Expert readers adapt their reading to the style of the text, an ability acquired through extensive reading and the study of texts and contexts of different periods. Perhaps the best example of this can be seen in the difference between how experts and novices respond to dialect. Because I teach and study regional and African American literature from the late nineteenth century, I have spent considerable time reading dialect, and I understand that a writer might use dialect to create atmosphere and to construct character and relationships. My students always struggle with dialect. They have little experience with this kind of writing and do not appreciate the value of this literary style. I can tell them why dialect is useful, but nothing I can tell them will make reading it easy. That has to come with practice. A similar level of linguistic comfort and critical understanding would allow a scholar of medieval literature to do the same with Middle English. The understanding that gives us this facility with language is difficult to explain to students, much less to teach. We know that the language of Chaucer, Shakespeare, or Charles Chesnutt will challenge our students, but we have few specific strategies to help them develop facility with unfamiliar languages.

Expert readers also recognize and know how to use a variety of literary concepts in interpreting a text. These include allusions, point of view, irony, and a wide array of formal elements. We don't just know what these terms mean or why they matter; we can also determine fairly easily which concept to use, we can apply it effectively, and we do this almost automatically. While our students may know the definitions of these concepts, and some may even apply them without prompting, they may not have the critical awareness to select the most appropriate concept or tool nor have the experience to use it well. They may be able to try different strategies, but many will do so only when prompted. The process can feel laborious, and students have sometimes complained that focusing on a particular strategy feels unnatural. In contrast, literary scholars usually use literary concepts unconsciously, moving from one to another intuitively, as we sense the value of trying a different approach or as we notice different features of the text. As with language, some of the difference is a matter of experience. Consider, for example, how familiarity with a large body of texts allows an expert reader to recognize allusions that someone who has simply read less might not even notice. Similarly, an expert reader can not only describe the point of view of a text but can also draw on knowledge of other texts to determine whether and how point of view affects the text's meaning and reception. In other words, these tools are deeply integrated with other aspects of our knowledge.

The ways that experts integrate content knowledge, appreciation of language, and various tools and concepts make clear that expert reading is an embedded and complex practice. Expert reading relies on the ability to notice features, draw on prior knowledge, and decode and interpret language and structures with relative ease. Consider again Scholes's example of reading the painting. In a mere three sentences, he shows how an expert might attend to half a dozen aspects of the text and its context, moving fluidly among them and his own interpretations. For an expert reader, paying attention to the text itself is essential, but it is not a first step in a clearly delineated series of discrete cognitive moves. It is, rather, embedded in a larger process of interpretation that involves several strategies and habits.

As Scholes's example shows, expert reading is inquisitive. Literary scholars notice features of the text and automatically frame questions about them and about their context, reception, and significance. Our questions attend to multiple levels, from details in the text to how the text reflects ideas about form, politics, and culture. Our habits of inquiry are shaped by our theoretical positions, which define why texts matter, how they work, and therefore how to approach them. Because we draw on different theories, we ask different kinds of questions. But regardless of the theoretical framework, reading involves active questioning. These questions are at once rhetorical, in the sense that we don't always expect to find answers, and generative. Our questions serve as keys to open the text or as frames to focus our reading.

Literary scholars are self-aware readers. We are conscious of the difference between our own experience and worldview, the culture in which the text was created, and the world represented in the text. It is this awareness combined with the historical, generic, and theoretical structures of the discipline that make expert reading comparative and connective. McCormick suggests that "the questions one asks of the text's history must necessarily come from one's position in the present." Because of this, she argues, "the absences one 'finds' are surely determined by the social formation in which the text is being read as well as the social formation in which it was written" (55). We read every new text through the lens of our prior reading of both literature and criticism. We notice features because they are similar to or different from what we've seen in other texts. The questions we pose are often about how one text connects with another (think of Scholes's questions about what the woman in the painting is reading, or if she is meant to be Mary) or about how a text reflects certain theoretical precepts. As Scholes notes, reading is an "intertextual activity." It is "never just the reduction of a text to some kernel of predetermined intention but always the connecting of signs in one text to other signs altogether" (2001 11). Expert readers make connections of multiple kinds: among texts, between texts and their authors, between text and context, and so on. The very structure of literary studies, with its emphasis on the history of literature, invites connective reading, and our ability to notice and consider relationships among texts relies on content knowledge. The habit of making such connections and the ability to sift through a massive body of knowledge to identify useful connections are both elements of strategic knowledge.

Literary scholars also read recursively. We move from noticing features to posing questions to making connections, and then back to the text itself, back to what we know about the context, back to theory, again and again. Scholes illustrates a key part of this process: taking provisional positions. Soon after noticing the key features of the painting, he writes, "Let us say . . . ," taking the provisional position that the book the woman is reading is the Bible. In a way, this kind of critical move treats the text as a logic puzzle, and the first step to solving the puzzle is to develop a hypothesis. Literary scholars develop such provisional interpretations habitually, even though we know that they may prove to be wrong. Literary hypotheses allow us to examine a text or problem through a particular lens, and we are comfortable revising or even abandoning our hypotheses as we continue to work with a text. As Randy Bass has suggested, one of the differences between expert and novice readers is that experts are able to both formulate hypotheses and defer reaching conclusions.[9] As Bass's argument reminds us, expert literary reading involves changing one's view of a text over time as one gains additional information, engages in conversation with others (whether in actual discussion or by reading critical analyses from other readers), and rethinks one's own responses. Literary scholars know, from experience, that our first conclusions are not likely to be our final ones, just as we know that the questions we begin with may well change as we continue reading. Any text we study, whether a four-line poem or a four-hundred-page novel, will require multiple readings before we're done. Indeed, one of the signs that students are developing literary expertise, I would argue, is that they come to understand the value of reading a text multiple times. For literary scholars, rereading continues long after we're apparently "done." Even with a completed analytical essay in hand, we know that the interpretation and analysis will continue to unfold through further research and conversations.

Protocols for Literary Argument

While this complex version of reading is the primary "method" of literary studies, the central practice of our discipline is argumentation. As Donald's description of literary studies suggests, the literary mindset includes awareness of and appreciation for the constructed, contentious nature of "truth" in the discipline, as well as habits of inquiry, research, and presentation that allow us to participate fully and effectively in disciplinary debates. Because we assume that texts do not have single or simple meanings, and because we value the discursive quality of literary scholarship, we are always aware that our own work, as both teachers and critics, is likely to be challenged or complicated by someone else's argument. Indeed, no matter how strongly we believe that our reading of a text is "correct," we know that it is shaped, as Donald notes, by the kinds of questions we have asked. While literary scholars may defend their positions fiercely, ultimately we understand our work as interpretive and therefore always open to further development and contradiction. In literary studies, there is (almost) no such thing as a definitive conclusion. We do not seek final answers. Rather, we participate in and extend a critical conversation.

Participating in these debates requires us to be adept at framing, pursuing, and presenting arguments that conform to the conventions of the discipline. While some aspects of this practice, such as properly citing and documenting sources or knowing about the various types of sources most often used in literary research, have been thoroughly discussed in textbooks and handbooks, much of the process is intuitive. Through practice and with guidance (in the form of critique) from graduate school advisors, peer reviewers, and journal editors, we have learned what kinds of questions are worth asking and how to develop and present persuasive arguments. While we can name the elements of literary research, in practice we rarely move predictably or neatly through them. Rather, we rely on intuition and serendipity, which are essential elements of our critical methodology. We can name the methodology, but it's difficult to describe, much less to teach, intuition and chance. We can name the elements of literary research and argument, but we have internalized and therefore don't usually describe the qualities that make for "good" analysis. We can say, for example, that a "good" argument explores a significant problem or observation, but what makes a problem "significant"? That is harder to define. The habits of mind that allow us to develop and present good literary arguments cannot be reduced to a checklist or a series of steps. They are the outward demonstration of our ways of thinking and reading; they are, at best, habits of mind made visible and concrete.

Knowing how to frame a worthwhile project—what questions to ask, what observations to explore, what problems to pose—illustrates the interdependence of content and strategic knowledge. In order to be significant and, therefore, worth pursuing, a project should offer a new reading of a text or group of texts. Better yet, the ideas we lay out should be applicable to other texts, or they might complicate existing ways of thinking about the period, genre, writer, or theory involved. Yet in order to do that, we must understand the existing critical discourse as well as the text(s) being studied. Good scholarship relies on content knowledge. It also relies on the scholar having internalized a way of thinking about literary problems, a critical stance that is developed through participation in critical conversation—in class discussions, critical articles, conference panels, and chats with colleagues. Furthermore, ways of thinking about literature change over time, as different theories and approaches gain or lose ground within the discipline.

Similarly, experience gives us a kind of scholarly intuition about what sources to examine. Experience teaches us how to know when we've read enough, how to recognize a gap in our research, and what kind of information might best fill the gap (or how to exploit the gap in making an argument), and what requires careful reading versus what we might simply scan. Because scholarly expertise develops through practice, effective research is difficult to teach and to learn. Nothing I can tell students will help them as much as experience will. Good research is also highly situational. Different questions demand different kinds of sources, and what one needs to learn for any given project depends on what one already knows. Literary scholars can navigate this uncertain terrain because they have strategically organized mental maps of criticism and types of sources. While the English curriculum makes visible a map of literary and cultural history and a map of literary concepts, the landscapes of criticism and research are less visible to both students and us, and we reference them less overtly and less often.

Our mental maps of the critical landscape facilitate both the selection of critical materials and our interactions with and uses of them. We select articles and books because we know, or think we know, how they will add to our understanding of a problem. We come to the scholarly text with fairly well-defined expectations and needs, because of our experience with research and analysis of a particular kind. We also come as informed readers. We may know something about the author's other work, or a title or a phrase early in a paper may signal how a piece fits into the critical landscape. Such signals help to show us how to approach a critical work, telling us what to expect and suggesting ways of reading. Knowing the critical debates is a matter of content knowledge; reading intentionally, knowing what to expect from a particular author, and being able to recognize tropes and terms as flags of allegiance to various approaches or theories are matters of strategic knowledge.

In addition to our prior knowledge of the critical landscape, critical sources require a specialized kind of reading. Students often assume that their difficulties in reading critical articles come from the academic writing style. They are partially right, of course. Academic prose can be turgid, obtuse, and full of jargon. For experts who read such writing regularly and who may write in that style, academic prose might be described as complex, playful, and specialized. No doubt, our facility with language and familiarity with critical writing make the academic style more accessible to us than it is to many of our students. But style is only part of the story. What allows scholars to read criticism fluently is our understanding of how critical arguments work. Along with a linguistic vocabulary, we have a rhetorical vocabulary. We recognize standard rhetorical strategies, such as beginning with an extended story or case that raises significant questions but that is not, in fact, the focus of the article, or structuring an article as an exploration of a problem or question and presenting a thesis near the end.[10]

The ability to read criticism well is reinforced by experience with writing it, and we learn to write effective literary arguments in part by imitating what we have read. Our abilities are refined with the help of the feedback we receive from peers and editors, whose responses to our work provide a form of coaching. Over time, we learn how to use primary and secondary sources effectively and how to organize an essay that is, at best, both engaging and complex. We learn not only to follow the conventions of the field but to use them with grace. We learn to deploy them to create interest and to strengthen an argument. In other words, we develop a scholarly voice, one that feels natural and even personal.

Strategic Knowledge and the English Major

None of what I've just described should be surprising. Much of it may seem like common sense, but, as Wineburg, Bransford, and others have suggested, what seems obvious to us may not even be visible to our students. No doubt, these elements of literary thinking are reflected in our English courses, and we may even discuss them overtly. But a look at the English curriculum suggests a tension between our belief that ways of thinking matter and how we organize students' learning. We proclaim the value of strategic knowledge, but in most colleges and universities, the English major focuses almost entirely on content.

If strategic knowledge is necessary for literary thinking, then it should be a primary focus, together with content knowledge, in the English curriculum. But a tour through English department websites, course listings, and professional debates in various MLA publications presents a muddled, even contradictory view of the place of strategic knowledge in the English curriculum. When we describe the value of the English major on websites and in university bulletins, we emphasize strategic knowledge. Few departments even mention the value of knowledge about literary history, different kinds of texts, or literary theory. Instead, we tout the critical thinking and communications skills that English majors gain. For example, on the opening page of its department website, the English department at Swarthmore College acknowledges the breadth of literary content it offers but emphasizes how the program develops students' abilities as readers and writers: "Whatever the classroom subject—from the details of a Shakespearean sonnet to the drama of Sam Shepard, from the fine-tuning of an argument on *Beloved* to a feminist critique of Milton—we hope to nurture imaginative reading, insightful analysis, cogent argument, and compelling prose." Similarly, the "guiding principles" of the English major at Montclair State University emphasize helping students "to develop their critical thinking abilities" and "to pay disciplined, informed, and appreciative attention to language, literature, film, and their own writing" (qtd. in Schwartz 19). In her book *Teaching Literature*, Elaine Showalter provides a list of the things she thinks English majors need to learn, beginning with "[h]ow to recognize subtle and complex differences in language use" and "[h]ow to read figurative language and distinguish between literal and metaphorical meaning" (26). Indeed, every item on her list begins with "how to"; there is no mention of the content knowledge of literary history in and of itself, although she emphasizes some uses of knowledge about literary history: "[h]ow to relate apparently disparate works to one another, and to synthesize ideas that connect them into a tradition or a literary period" (27). English faculty echo this emphasis on helping students learn how to think about literature rather than on acquiring specific knowledge about a specific period or genre. One faculty member explained that she wants students to learn "to see the bricks being laid rather than the finished structure," in part because "[seeing] how the ideas are being constructed" would help students understand better how to formulate their own ideas, arguments, and lives. Another commented that she tries "to help students not only understand what they read but also be able to write a persuasive argument." As these examples suggest, much of what we say about studying English focuses on ways of thinking about literature, rather than on content knowledge. Our statements about the purpose of the English major suggest that, as a field, we have, as Scholes suggested, stopped "thinking of ourselves as if we had a subject matter and start[ed] thinking of ourselves as having a discipline which we can offer our students as part of the cultural equipment that they are going to need when they leave us" (1998 67).

Yet our belief in the centrality of strategic knowledge does not seem to have shaped the curriculum. With few exceptions, most notably in descriptions of introductory courses, English curricula pay little overt attention to the development of students' literary thinking abilities. Literary history remains central, though with less emphasis on comprehensive coverage. Departments generally require students to take courses in literature from different periods and perspectives, usually including early British literature, British and American literature after 1800, and some multicultural requirement. Most programs require an introductory course in literary studies that introduces literary terms, conventions of writing about literature, the major genres (novel, short story, poem, play), and the basics of literary research. Many programs ask students to take a course in linguistics, writing, theory, or criticism. Some departments allow students significant individual choice, relying heavily on electives or distribution requirements, while others have tighter structures and offer less choice. While the contemporary curriculum has expanded to include non-mainstream writers and concerns, popular literature, and nonliterary genres—such as photography and television—traditional literary history remains the core of the English major. As W. B. Carnochan wrote in a 2000 essay surveying changes in the English major over time, "Literature and the greats are still with us, conspicuously so, notwithstanding doomsayers who claim to believe that everything important has been replaced by ephemera" (1959). Literary history, including the traditional canon, remains the organizing scheme and thus the apparent focus of the English major.

Content knowledge dominates in course listings and descriptions as well. Most departments offer similar core courses focused on periods, genres, and writers: Shakespeare, The Modern Novel, Twentieth-Century American Poetry. These "standard" courses are complemented with topics courses that allow professors and students the freedom to explore alternative materials and approaches: women's autobiography, queer fiction, literature about medicine. The range of topics courses is not, however, as diverse nor as clearly contested as one might expect from a discipline that takes pride in its divergence. Courses on women's writing, postcolonial literature, literatures by people of color, gay and lesbian literature, and "reading" nonliterary texts exist on many—if not most—campuses. These courses may be the result of disciplinary debates about what literature scholars ought to study, but they have not, as Carnochan notes, supplanted traditional approaches.

Further, the structure of the English major is rarely designed to support students' learning. Because the focus is on the coverage of content rather than on the development of expertise, most departments organize the major around required courses or categories, with little attention to the order in which courses are taken. Experts on learning argue that people develop both strategic and content knowledge by building new understanding on the foundation of prior learning. This would suggest the value of organizing a curriculum so that students move in some logical sequence to build understanding over time. The English major typically has a beginning requirement, usually a course that introduces the core strategic knowledge of literary studies, and some programs have a capstone that, in theory at least, synthesizes students' learning. In between, students in most programs select whatever courses they wish, fulfilling a set of distribution and elective requirements but not moving through courses in a specific order. This open structure reflects the nature of the field, as well as practical considerations such as scheduling, but it may create difficulty for students. Consider the range of experience and diversity of background knowledge of a typical group of students in an advanced literature course: some will have just completed the introductory course, while others are preparing to graduate. These students know different literary content and have different levels of strategic knowledge. Not only are the less-experienced students likely to be less-skilled readers, they also have less well-developed skills in literary research and writing. Rather than attending to students' developing knowledge or their different levels of preparation, abilities, and needs, we treat them all the same. This doesn't prevent students from developing content and strategic knowledge over the course of the major, but they may accomplish this despite the structure of the major, not because of it.

The curriculum might look quite different if we focused more on developing students' abilities and provided more developmental structure. Lucy Cromwell describes how the English curriculum at Alverno College guides students from a beginner phase, during which they are encouraged to move from reading for the story to considering specific elements of the text, to an intermediate stage of going "beyond analysis of discrete elements to make connections and infer relationships" and learning "the components of several significant literary frameworks." During their junior year, students begin to apply those frameworks in their own responses and analyses, but with direction from faculty (84). In the advanced stage, during their senior year, students select and develop their own versions of those (or other) theoretical approaches. At the advanced stage, "students bring together discrete pieces of literary analysis and response and learn to infer patterns from their reading. . . . they learn to make connections and see how they are building interpretation. . . . They develop the ability to let the work suggest possibilities of meaning" (85). By focusing on students' developing abilities, rather than on the coverage of different aspects of literary studies, the Alverno model emphasizes strategic knowledge.

But it is the exception. At present, and probably for the foreseeable future, the English curriculum remains focused on the coverage of literary history and genres. Our requirements and the structure of the major encourage students to learn content knowledge, and they downplay the development of strategic knowledge. It's not that we don't recognize or value strategic knowledge, however. In my survey of literature faculty, most report that they both address strategic knowledge and view it as central in the curriculum. Over 80 percent indicate that they teach students to recognize literary devices, how to apply theoretical concepts, and how to develop effective literary arguments. More than half report teaching about how to deal with unfamiliar language or how to resolve difficulties in interpreting a text, though these are judged as less central to the curriculum. Yet the evidence also suggests that we provide too little overt instruction on elements of strategic knowledge. For example, while literature faculty indicate that one of the things they most want students to learn is how to make literary arguments, and the research paper appears to be the most common assignment in advanced English courses, few programs or syllabi appear to give much direct attention to helping students learn to write literary arguments. Well over half of the faculty surveyed report that they always require students to write research papers, but outside of introductory courses, almost no one teaches students how to do literary research or write literary arguments. The assumption appears to be that students either will learn everything they need to know in the introductory course, which seems unlikely, or that they will develop their literary research and argument skills through practice, with minimal guidance or feedback.

This apparent contradiction reflects a core belief that students develop strategic knowledge by listening to lectures and participating in class discussions. Lecture and discussion are the *signature pedagogies* of literary studies, to use the term invented by Lee Shulman to refer to a discipline's standard pedagogical practices. In lectures, we provide background information, explain our analyses of texts, and direct students' attention to the significant features of literary movements, genres, texts, and theories. This may involve some back-and-forth with students, but a lecture is usually structured around the professor's preferred way of reading a text, and the goal is to transmit our knowledge about and interpretation of the text to our students. In doing so, we might explain the key critical perspectives that guide our interpretations or cite critical analyses, historical information, and other sources that contribute to our views. Lectures are, essentially, informal, conversational versions of the literary arguments we make in our scholarly writing. But while most lectures make visible the logic behind a reading of a text, they also highlight the end product of a long, complex thinking process rather than the process itself. Students don't hear or see how we developed our analyses. We share interpretations, but we usually don't talk about how the insight that sparked the interpretation came to us, nor about how it developed. We offer evidence, but we don't explain how we found it or how we knew that it was relevant. Our thinking processes remain in the background, almost entirely hidden from view, and almost never explained.

The other dominant mode of literary teaching is class discussion. While some faculty approach discussion in wide-open ways, beginning with the question "What did you think of this?" and pursuing the discussion in any direction students wish to go, most English faculty structure discussions more deliberately. We pose questions that are designed to engage students in looking at texts in specific ways. Through this process, students practice literary ways of thinking. Still, even as we lead critical discussions, we rarely provide guidance about how to determine what questions to ask or where to look in the text, in other literary works, in the critical literature, and in the historical context to develop good answers. We recognize "good" answers, and we often highlight them when students offer them in discussions, but we don't always make clear why some responses are "good" and others less useful. Discussion requires students to use strategic knowledge, but it doesn't necessarily provide any overt advice about how to deploy such knowledge, nor does it encourage students to consider what kinds of strategic knowledge they are using or to evaluate their own strategies. The assumption is that students will learn all of this indirectly, through experience.

These approaches to teaching literature reflect the nature of our discipline, and Shulman suggests that this is typical of signature pedagogies. Just as the adversarial question-and-debate of the law classroom prepares students for the courtroom, literary pedagogies echo the core practices of our discipline. Literary thinking relies heavily on reading between the lines and determining meaning that is not obvious or clearly mapped out. Our teaching methods require our students to locate or "read" the strategic knowledge of literary study in much the same way we want them to read texts: by identifying patterns, recognizing subtle connections, and noticing key ideas that might or might not be emphasized. The difference is that in class we draw their attention to textual matters; we leave the thinking processes implicit.

Our expectations about student learning are similar to our ideas about interpreting texts: just as the meanings of a text may not reside on the surface but instead be embedded in the combination of content, form, and context, so too is strategic knowledge often embedded in classroom presentations and conversations. Our overt focus in teaching is usually on understanding the text, not on the literary thinking involved in interpretation. We take the time to draw students' attention to how the sonnet form connects with a poem's meaning, but we rarely highlight the thinking processes involved in noticing and interpreting form. As literary critics, we rely on the disciplinary practices of reading between the lines and against the grain to interpret texts. But is it reasonable to expect students, who are in the process of learning literary thinking, to "read between the lines" in order to notice the strategic knowledge involved in our classroom discourse?

The typical teaching strategies of our discipline suggest that this is exactly what we expect students to do. I see two problems with this belief. The first is that it presents literary interpretation as a form of magic, rather than as a discipline or craft. When we lay out the necessary background knowledge, direct students' attention to the most significant aspects of a text, and lead them through a discussion that reveals the interpretation we developed through hours of analysis and research, we help them understand the meaning and significance of a text, but we may not be helping them learn to develop their own interpretations. As Scholes argues, our refusal to "give up our claims to special status as interpreters of quasi-sacred texts" or to let go of ownership of "the magical powers of literary theory" creates a "gap between our pedagogical practices and the needs of our students." We should, he claims, "rethink our practice by starting with the needs of our students rather than with our inherited professionalism or our personal preferences" (2001 83–84). Our habit of presenting fully formed interpretations, or even of carefully guiding students to them through discussion, may account for students' lack of confidence when presented with an unfamiliar text. Rather than deploying the analytical strategies they were supposed to be learning through class discussions, students believe that they must rely on experts to begin work on new texts or problems. While they may well have acquired some strategic knowledge, it seems that they have also learned that they are not capable of interpreting literature on their own. Of course, we want them to understand the value of criticism, but surely we also want them to trust themselves as readers.

My second concern with the assumption that students will develop literary thinking through indirect exposure is that it just doesn't work for many of them. In students' eyes, the literature curriculum lacks not only coherence but also a core set of ideas and practices. Beyond a general understanding that literature is connected with history, students identify almost no connections among their courses. Some report acquiring the habit and ability to compare a new text with ones they've read previously, and many say that their research and writing skills improved, but almost none could identify anything they had learned in one course that would apply to others. The very idea that they were acquiring skills and strategies instead of simply exploring the literature of different periods seemed surprising to them. If, as Bransford et al. suggest, expertise includes metacognition and adaptability, then it is in our students' interest for them to not only learn but also be consciously aware that the strategic knowledge they use to analyze *Beowulf* can also help them interpret *Beloved*.

Some will argue that typical teaching methods in literature courses would work perfectly well, if only students would either work hard enough or come into the classroom as better readers. Because the habits of mind of literary interpretation seem natural to us, and because our best students seem to develop literary thinking skills easily, we assume that our teaching methods are effective, and so we believe that the problem is not our teaching but our students' lack of effort or ability. Rather than brushing the problem aside as a flaw in the students, we should consider that many of our students don't "get it" because we keep "it" hidden. If we only gesture in the direction of literary thinking, rather than presenting strategic knowledge directly, many of our students will never learn how to use it.

It is not enough, I believe, for students to learn about the history of literature and the relationship between literature and history, though these are central themes in most of my courses. I want them to understand how to frame a good historical question and how to explore that question appropriately. It's not enough for them to be familiar with several varieties of literary theory, nor is it sufficient for them to be able to read reasonably well. I want them to be aware of the range of theoretical and critical options available to them so that they can evaluate and adjust their approaches. I believe that making strategic knowledge visible will help all of our students, those who are struggling as well as those for whom literary thinking seems easy. As Wineburg suggests, teaching students some basic strategies for interpretation can empower them to develop their own smart interpretations, rather than relying on SparkNotes or class discussions or the words of critics or teachers to tell them how to read a text. The key is teaching the craft of literary interpretation, rather than dazzling students with our interpretations or leading them along a predetermined path to an interpretation without pointing out how we constructed the path in the first place. According to *How People Learn,* research on learning "suggests that novices might benefit from models of how experts approach problem solving—especially if they receive coaching in using similar strategies" (30). Scholes writes that we should not be "artisans shaping the impressionable minds of our students. We are—or should be—masters of our craft helping others to master it" (2001 68). In *The Rise and Fall of English,* he argues that we can best accomplish this by completely overhauling the literature curriculum. We should, he suggests, "replace the canon of texts with a canon of methods" (1998 145). While I find his proposal appealing, I don't believe that it's realistic or necessary. We can improve students' learning of literary methods without a complete curricular makeover. Strategic thinking is already present in our classrooms. The task before us is to help students recognize its presence between the lines of elegant lectures and engaging discussions and then to guide them as they begin to use it on their own.

2 ▪ Making Literary Thinking Visible

A confession: I'm sometimes—OK, often—pretty laid-back about preparing for class. Like many long-time teachers, I teach some core texts regularly, and I rely on a few tried-and-true teaching methods. So if I've been sick, or very busy, or just plain lazy, I know that I can go into class and teach the first session on, say, the poetry of Paul Laurence Dunbar without notes. Because language can be an obstacle in Dunbar's work but is also central to its significance, we always begin by reading "When Malindy Sings," one of Dunbar's "dialect poems," out loud. I want students to get their mouths around the musical sounds of the poem and to connect what look like unfamiliar clusters of letters to very familiar words. We talk about why the poem is difficult to read, about how Dunbar's dialect can be hard to decipher but how, once you begin to hear the rhythm and the accent, it becomes clear. Then, I ask students to work on specific critical tasks in small groups. One group focuses on describing the speaker of the poem, while another considers who they think the speaker is addressing. Yet another discusses how readers at the turn of the nineteenth century might have responded to the poem. I remind everyone to be prepared to provide evidence for their ideas, either from the poem or from our earlier class discussions and readings. I also encourage each group to present multiple answers to the questions I pose, to embrace their members' different views rather than focus on reaching consensus. After a while, the groups report on their discussions, and I invite others to respond by offering additional evidence, suggesting other interpretations, or identifying connections with their own group's task. Usually, we run out of time, and at least one group has to wait until the next day.

By this point in my teaching career, I have a clear sense of how reading Dunbar fits into the larger course, and I know what kinds of issues the poem's dialect will raise. Dunbar's poems have become a kind of set piece, an old standard in my repertoire. So, too, are the small groups. I use them almost every day, to the point that students sometimes tease me about it. The group conversations achieve two things: first, they ensure that I don't just tell students what I think (and therefore what they should think), and second, working in small groups on concrete tasks requires students to look closely at the text, draw on what they've already learned, and develop informal arguments and support them with concrete evidence. I like how they work, but they've also become habits.

Like thinking about literature, teaching about literature becomes habitual if you do it long enough. To a great extent, we teach the way we were taught, but even professors who have adopted pedagogies quite different from those we experienced tend to embrace a particular approach and stick with it. We adopt these habits because they are comfortable and because we believe they work. We may come to our teaching styles without careful analysis, most often simply by imitating how we were taught or by doing what feels "natural," and we keep teaching that way because we're satisfied with the results.

For many literature faculty, the traditional pedagogy of the field seems perfectly adequate. It worked for us, after all. Randy Bass describes how he developed the habit of teaching "mostly the way I had been taught, and tended to replicate the pedagogies that worked best—quite frankly—on *me* (or slight variations of me)" (1999 4). Nancy Chick calls this "pedagogical narcissism" (10). The combination of lecture and guided discussion that occurs in most literature classrooms, combined with the more intense guidance the luckiest of us received from our advisors and dissertation readers, helped us acquire the habits of mind as well as the content knowledge required to join the professional discussions of our discipline. Inspired by the dazzling performances of our best professors (and informed even by the merely functional), we give lectures that present our students with fully developed analyses, or we guide students through discussions that lead them to the very interpretation we find most persuasive. In her essay describing the "signature pedagogy" of literary studies, Chick describes this type of teaching as "professorial packing." Not only in lectures but even in the guise of class discussions or providing appropriate background information, we present our predetermined interpretations. It is usually only indirectly that we help students develop the ability to interpret texts on their own (10–11).

Many of us assume that this works, again because it worked for us. We read lively class discussions as evidence that students understand the ideas we're presenting. We view good research papers on topics related to the course material as evidence that students understand the issues, themes, and approaches of the course. The danger is that we are all, as Grant Wiggins has argued, prone to self-deception: "How easily we hear what we want and need to hear in a student answer or question; how quickly we assume that if a few intelligent comments are made, all students get the point" (qtd. in Bass 1999 5). We want to believe that covering content, presenting our interpretations, and guiding students to predetermined readings teach students how to think well about literature, but these approaches may not be working for all of our students. When we perform a critical reading through lecture or guided discussion, we may demonstrate the application of literary thinking, but we don't teach students how to do it themselves. Lectures work well to introduce concepts and strategies but don't necessarily enable students to use them; discussions and other "student-centered" techniques can leave students without the knowledge they need to perform their own critical readings. The problem does not lie in lecturing or discussion as pedagogical genres though.

The problem is that too much of our thinking about teaching focuses on us, even when we're designing "student-centered" courses, in part because we don't have a clear vision of what English majors really need to learn. Of course, our students will use what they learn in quite different ways. Those who pursue graduate study may need to learn the outline of literary history and key ideas of literary theories, the foundation of the discipline. But many other English majors will not go on to graduate school, and most will not become literary scholars. For those who will work in business and other nonliterary fields, the content knowledge of the field is ultimately less useful than our strategic knowledge. What they need is exactly what so many of our descriptions of the English major promise: to develop the ability to read, interpret, and create texts of various kinds; to learn about how human beings and their societies work, including how expressive texts provide insight into human experience; and to develop the ability to make connections and comparisons among different periods, texts, approaches, and ideas—or, as the cliché would have it, to develop critical thinking skills. Knowing the difference between iambic pentameter and free verse may not help a college graduate succeed in business, but knowing how to analyze the structure of an argument or think critically about the relationship between audience, purpose, and context will. Moreover, our students need what Bransford and his colleagues call "adaptive expertise," the ability to adjust their approaches to meet the challenges of new situations. These skills are also useful for those who go on to graduate school, of course, for they will have to deploy strategic knowledge in their research and teaching. Put simply, strategic knowledge is the most practical and useful outcome of the English major.

While we promote the practical value of literary study, what really draws most of us and our students to English are the pleasures of reading and the insights literature offers into perspectives, experiences, and stories that help us understand the world and ourselves. Focusing on approaches and methods might seem formulaic, unrelated to the seemingly intuitive process of finding meaning that we so enjoy, but that process is, I would argue, facilitated by strategic knowledge. We appreciate and learn from literature because we know how to read it well. Strategic knowledge helps us engage deeply and productively with literary texts, and that in turn inspires our passion for literature. It can do the same for our students.

After all, presenting our textual passions does not always foster an echoing passion among our students. Professorial enthusiasm is often not sufficient to make poems by Tennyson or Cotton Mather's sermons appealing to twenty-year-olds who love Tolkien and Chuck Palahniuk. Of course, our purpose is not to persuade students to like the texts we treasure, but we do want to equip them to understand and appreciate the significance of those texts. When students acquire interpretive tools, they gain confidence in their ability to tackle difficult texts, and that has its own pleasures. Students may not come to love all of the texts that we love, but they recognize the value of developing their skills as readers and interpreters. To help my students develop their literary thinking skills, gain confidence in their own interpretive abilities, and engage productively with difficult texts, I have adapted the model of *cognitive apprenticeship,* which casts learning as a process of acquiring and internalizing expert ways of thinking.

" cognitive apprenticeship "

Students as Apprentices

Educational researchers Allan Collins, John Seely Brown, and Susan E. Newman suggest that we think of learning as a form of apprenticeship, in which students learn ways of thinking in much the same way that people learn practical physical skills like how to throw a baseball or make a quilt. Based on the process of training novices in skilled trades, cognitive apprenticeship begins with observation, as students watch an expert perform the task. This helps them develop a conceptual model of what they are learning to do. They begin practicing the task in simple ways, with an expert guiding them through the process, and they receive constructive criticism and feedback as they practice. Over time, as the students gain facility, the expert provides less guidance and feedback, fading into the background. I have found that, through this kind of cognitive apprenticeship, my students not only build their strategic knowledge but also gain awareness of and confidence in their own abilities. As Collins, Brown, and Newman explain, the process helps students develop an "internalized guide" for whatever cognitive practices they are learning; they develop the ability to monitor and improve their own performance.

Thinking in these terms shifts the emphasis in literature classes. A course may focus on specific texts, periods, genres, and themes, but within that content-oriented framework, we can also discuss and practice using various strategies for reading, analyzing, and researching literature. When I teach Dunbar, for example, we talk about how this poet might have been influenced by his cultural context, and we consider multiple ways of thinking about dialect poems. We discuss how the poems reflect the politics of race, poetic form, performance, and social class. But Dunbar's poems also offer opportunities for students to practice strategies for dealing with difficult language, to develop a vocabulary of inquiry that allows them to move from uncertainty into provisional readings, to learn how to make their own connections between critical and historical sources and literary texts, and to construct persuasive literary arguments. For each of these literary tools, I introduce the concept, show them how it works, lead them through some initial practice, ask them to practice on their own, and provide feedback on their efforts. For example, I bring in a few historical and critical sources, and we discuss how they help us understand Dunbar's poems. We also talk about how different types of sources provide different kinds of insight. I then ask students to locate additional relevant sources and discuss what they contribute to our analysis of the poems. In other words, Dunbar's poems both help students learn about literary history and provide a chance to learn and practice specific ways of studying literature. When students begin to practice strategic knowledge, discussions of texts focus increasingly on their interpretations, rather than on mine. By helping students develop their literary thinking skills, we help them acquire the ability and confidence to analyze independently. Built into this approach are two key elements of cognitive apprenticeship: modeling and scaffolding.

Modeling

The first step in cognitive apprenticeship is *modeling*, which involves not simply performing a critical task in front of students but actively demonstrating the process. Think of the way the chef on a television cooking program describes the process of making a soufflé. We don't simply see the steps he takes, we also hear his explanation of what he is doing and why. A typical classroom lecture would be something like watching the cooking show with the sound turned off. We see the chef's moves but we don't hear the commentary. In class, we often present the results of our own analysis of a literary text or problem without explaining the thinking processes that led us to that analysis. Consider this description of Diane Middlebrook's lecture on T. S. Eliot's "The Love Song of J. Alfred Prufrock":

Middlebrook also "pulls out the pronoun moments" and emphasizes the role of the implied listener: "'Let us go then, you and I.' Who is the 'you'?" An answer lies within the poem, and by the end of the process, Middlebrook hopes students will see that the fragmented subjectivity of the narrator makes You and I both parts of himself. By the ending—"Human voices wake us and we drown"—I and you can come together. (qtd. in Showalter 68)

Here, Middlebrook draws students' attention to moments in the text that she believes hold the key to its meaning. She raises literary questions about the poem, and she presents her answers to them. In the process, she shows students her interpretation of the poem. What she does not do, at least according to this précis of her lecture, is explain to students how she knew which moments in the poem would be most useful, why she decided to ask questions about the speaker and the auditor, or why the pronoun shift stood out as significant. No doubt, the lecture described here would be engaging, and students would gain insight into the poem by listening to Middlebrook's journey through the text. A few might notice and remember the critical moves that Middlebrook made and try them out with the next poem they read, but it's equally possible that most would feel just as unsure about how to wrestle with an unfamiliar poem as they were before they heard the lecture.

It would take only a slight shift for this lecture to serve as both a guided tour of the poem and a useful demonstration of how to interpret poetry. Imagine if the lecturer stopped a few times during the presentation to draw students' attention to her critical moves, perhaps to name them as strategies or remind students that she had used a similar approach with a poem she explicated last week. Instead of simply raising the question "Who is the 'you'?" she might talk about why she poses that kind of question, about how a text might have both a speaker and an implied auditor, or about how focusing on the auditor led her to notice significant aspects of the poem. We may assume that students already know these things, whether from introductory literature courses or from reading experience, or that they will figure them out by listening to good lectures, but given the widely acknowledged difficulty that even advanced students have with poetry, neither of these assumptions seems accurate. If I don't draw students' attention to strategy, both they and I are likely to keep our focus on the content. Stopping to comment on the process makes visible the internal dialogue that occurs in most critical thinking. Showing our thinking helps students develop conceptual models of interpretive strategies.

Scaffolding

Hearing the TV chef explain how to whip egg whites to the proper stiffness doesn't mean that I can make a good soufflé the first time I try. If I want to get it right, I have to practice. The same applies to literary thinking. As Robert Scholes argues:

> The knowledge that we retain is the knowledge that we can and do employ. . . . What we take in through our eyes and ears must emerge from our hands and mouths if we are to hold on to it. It is a curious property of information that we keep it only if we give it away. Material "covered" in classrooms and not incorporated into the communicative lives of students simply fades away. (1998 148–149)

Courses that rely solely on lectures provide little opportunity for practice, except in student papers and essay exams. Discussion-centered courses provide more opportunities, though not all discussion develops students' strategic knowledge. We can build opportunities for practice into class discussions through *scaffolding*. Like the scaffolds that brick-layers use as they build high walls, cognitive scaffolding supports students as they build their interpretations and literary thinking abilities. While any question or prompt will shape a class discussion, the most effective scaffolding guides students in how to think. Open-ended questions and personal response questions may prime the discussion pump, but if we want students to learn how to analyze literature, we need to be more directive. We should pose questions that require students to practice using specific literary concepts or frameworks. Scaffolding can also guide students through the process of exploring an issue or text, suggesting not just an initial question but also strategies for considering multiple angles, testing hypotheses, and developing ideas.

Repetition and variation help students develop their literary thinking skills. Each time students work on contextualizing a text or applying a particular theory, they become more adept. When students begin to use these strategies on new texts, they begin to develop the ability to adapt their skills to new situations. I usually ask students to work with an analytical tool multiple times over the course of several class meetings, and we often move from a full-class discussion using a strategy, to small-group work, to individual writing. As we move through these multiple rounds, I provide less guidance over time. For example, I might introduce the concept of poetic structure by asking students to describe the structure of a poem we're reading and to discuss how the structure supports and challenges the poem's meanings. At that point, I would guide the discussion forcefully to ensure that the idea is clear. The next day, I might ask students to work in small groups to identify and discuss the structure of other poems, and, as a class, we would compare their findings. As we discussed the poems, we would develop a list of different types of structures or the various ways that structure intersects with other aspects of each poem. In a journal assignment, I might then ask them to choose another poem and write about its structure, using the list we generated. A few days later, we might begin to apply the concept of structure to our discussion of a short story or novel.

No doubt, this approach takes time. I could, of course, just give an excellent lecture on poetic structure and move on. But while I want students to understand structure conceptually and see how it works in different texts, I also want them to develop the ability to notice, describe, and analyze structure on their own. In order to achieve this, I ask them not only to practice reading for structure but also to identify structural patterns across different texts, so that they develop and expand their vocabulary for talking about structure. By taking the time to have students work with the concept in multiple ways, I can help them learn both why structure matters and how to use it themselves.

Scaffolding breaks down the complex, intuitive process of literary analysis into concrete steps, and that can seem to define literary thinking in overly simple or overly technical ways. When I first began working with cognitive apprenticeship, I resisted the idea of making a list of steps or questions, because I valued the creativity and complexity of the interdisciplinary ways of thinking that I wanted students to learn. If I defined interdisciplinary analysis as a set of concrete steps, I feared that those qualities would be lost. What I discovered, however, is that students were actually better able to develop creative, complex analyses if I provided them with clear instructions and guided them through the process. When students began with a simple analysis of a short text, then brought in other texts for comparison, and finally identified how the texts reflected their cultural contexts, their work improved dramatically. Scaffolding showed them how to weave diverse elements together, because it made the process simple, linear, and visible. Instead of leaving students with an overly simple understanding of interdisciplinary thinking, the incremental approach prepared them to create their own variations and move toward more sophisticated, expert integrative interpretations.[1] The scaffold did exactly what the bricklayers' scaffold does: it provided a simple utilitarian frame that allowed students to slowly build more complex and sturdy structures. Research on learning indicates that my students' experience is typical. In a study of how experts develop intuitive thinking, Hubert L. Dreyfus and Stuart E. Dreyfus found that providing learners with guidance early on allows them to gain the experience necessary to develop the expertise for improvisation. As Michael Carter explains, citing the Dreyfus and Dreyfus study, "without *some* guidance, a novice would never be able to become an expert" (272).

I'm not saying that every class discussion must be entirely focused on practicing literary thinking. Nor do I believe that questions that invite students to use strategic knowledge cannot at the same time engage students or generate productive and exciting discussions. Quite the contrary. The discussions that ensue from carefully structured opportunities for students to practice literary thinking strategies are usually lively, interesting, and productive. The process of developing their own answers to literary problems excites students and engages them intellectually.

Putting It All Together

Through modeling and scaffolding, we can make visible literary knowledge that is both complex and intuitive. Not only can cognitive apprenticeship help students develop their strategic knowledge, it can also help make that learning transferable. When we draw attention to the methods and habits of mind we use to analyze contemporary film or poetry, we encourage students to recognize that those approaches could be useful in interpreting a seventeenth-century play or an eighteenth-century essay. By modeling literary thinking strategies and providing guidance as students practice them, we can help students build their own repertoires of critical tools. We can also help students learn to be discerning about selecting which tool to use for a particular literary problem and enhance their ability to monitor and adapt their approaches as they work. Building modeling and scaffolding into courses is not difficult, but we will have to think differently about what we're doing in order to make it work.

Modeling the Use of Cognitive Apprenticeship

Just as when I teach students how to wrestle with dialect or think about poetic structure, the best way to make clear how cognitive apprenticeship works may be first to model and then to scaffold the process. In some ways, modeling literary thinking requires only a slight change in classroom practices, but incorporating modeling into my teaching has made me more aware of what students need to learn and more deliberate about explaining strategic thinking.

Making Complexity Visible

Among the greatest challenges in teaching literature is helping students develop complex analyses that integrate texts, contexts, and theories. Students recognize that literature reflects its context, but they often have difficulty identifying and using relevant contextual information. In much of their experience, context and theory are givens—that is, faculty provide the background information and draw on their own preferred theories. I want students to develop the ability to locate and use contextual sources on their own and to make conscious choices among theoretical approaches.

As I was beginning to learn about cognitive apprenticeship, I developed two multimedia projects that I hoped would model historically based literary criticism. My first attempt at deliberate modeling mostly failed, but I hope that it will serve as an instructive example of what not to do. Because I had found that students struggled to frame research questions, to connect texts with their historical contexts in meaningful ways, and to use primary sources effectively, I wanted to make these thinking strategies visible. I was teaching a course called American Popular Narratives, so I created an online exhibit based on an article I'd published on "popular narratives" about the Swedish singer Jenny Lind. The exhibit provides a brief introduction to Lind, and it walks students through my research process, from my initial interest, to the kinds of materials I looked at, to the finished essay. I show and comment on excerpts from my research notes, lay out my research questions in several categories (e.g., questions about women's public roles in the middle of the nineteenth century, questions about why some public figures gain popularity), and describe the key insights that helped me move from exploring visual images of and press reports about Lind to developing an argument about how they worked. The exhibit ends with an annotated, color-coded version of the article, in which I try to show students where and how I used primary sources, critical sources, and theoretical concepts, as well as moments when all three were integrated.

"Reading Lindmania: Research and Argument" was an ambitious project, especially for someone who was learning both a new way of thinking about student learning and how to build a website. Setting aside the somewhat clunky graphic and technical design, the site failed on a pedagogical level. I had hoped that it would make elements of the research process visible and thus give students a clearer sense of how they might approach their own research projects. Instead, the site overwhelmed them, and it reinforced their existing impression that the purpose of research was to find the right answer. I felt like Prufrock: that was not what I meant at all.

Looking back at the site, I see why it failed. First, I tried to model too much at one time, which led me to gloss over some highly complex aspects of my own thinking process and intimidate rather than inform my students. At the same time, the exhibit makes the research process look neatly linear, which of course it never is. It provides little insight into the nuts and bolts of locating and selecting sources or how I knew what to focus on as I read them, much less how I came up with what were quite large research questions. I had tried to describe my thinking processes clearly, but the case I used was complex and quite unlike anything my students had ever done. Even though in many ways the exhibit oversimplified the real thinking involved in researching the article, it described a larger, more complex project than what I expected students to do in an undergraduate course. It left them confused and quite sure that they were not prepared to do the right kind of research, because it simply did not model the processes they most needed to understand.

In contrast, the other case I developed for that course worked better than I anticipated. In order to help students understand the idea that critical interpretation integrates aspects of texts, contexts, and theories, I asked them to analyze a thirty-second animated music video. I hoped that considering how images, sound, and narrative work together in the video would help them understand how texts, contexts, and theories work together in literary analysis. I asked students to view the video and then answer a series of questions about what made it funny.[2] After they first noted their own theories, students were directed to focus on the visual elements of the video. The "Alien Song" video features a one-eyed space alien, dressed in a unitard emblazoned with a one-eyed smiley face, dancing and lip-synching to Gloria Gaynor's version of "I Will Survive." I asked students to take note of whatever visual elements they noticed, but I also encouraged them to think about whether they'd ever seen similar images and to focus on details like the character's movements and clothing. Then, I directed their attention to the sound quality, asking them to compare the Gaynor version of the song with two other renditions. Next, I asked them to consider the song on the level of narrative: what "story" did it tell? This required them to think about both the lyrics—"I've got all my life to live, I've got all my love to give, and I'll survive, I will survive"—and the narrative path of the video, which ends with a glass-mosaic disco ball falling on the alien's head and killing him just as he mouths the last "I will survive." Finally, I asked students to consider how the visual, musical, and narrative elements fit together to make the video funny. In class, we added historical dimensions, brainstorming what we knew about disco, contemporary animation, and music videos. I explained the theory that humor is created by linguistic and narrative disruptions, things that violate our expectations, like the one-eyed smiley face and the falling disco ball, and we applied this to the video as well.

While all of this was entertaining and began to engage students in questions about what makes popular narratives tick, it also served as an effective analogy. As I explained in class, critical analysis of popular narratives is much like the video: meaning rests not in any single element but in the way the elements work together. Students enjoyed the exercise, but the analogy also made sense, in part because we had translated it into action in our class discussion: we drew on the text itself, on information about the historical context, and on theoretical concepts to develop our analysis of the video's humor. While the pleasure of playing with this silly video helped, as did starting with a pop culture text rather than a scholarly project, I think the key to the success of this attempt at modeling is that it was fairly modest, both in terms of what I was attempting to do and in terms of the scope of the case. Instead of trying to oversimplify a very complex process, the "Alien Song" exercise modeled one significant concept, and it did so in a style and language that built on students' existing knowledge. It also worked because it provided a conceptual model that students could reference and apply easily as they began to pursue their own research projects. As the course progressed, the music video analysis served as a template for more complex, multifaceted analyses.

My first forays into modeling taught me several useful lessons. One was simply not to take on too much. The whole research process could not be modeled effectively, but a single concept worked well. I also learned that modeling is not merely a matter of making my own thinking processes visible. Rather, the best modeling provides students with conceptual models that they can adapt and use. That is why concrete, relatively simple models work best. Finally, I gained respect for just how difficult it can be to describe my own ways of thinking, and I recognized how useful a model could be when it works.

Using Literary Concepts

While demonstrating literary ways of thinking can help students construct conceptual models to guide their work, the other half of the modeling and scaffolding process is perhaps even more useful. If we want students to internalize literary habits of mind, they need opportunities to practice. But, as Bourdieu argues, they need *guided* practice: "One can acquire the fundamental principles of a practice

. . . only by practicing it at the side of a sort of guide or trainer, who assures and reassures, who sets an example and makes corrections" (qtd. in Brubaker 230). We cannot sit by the side of each student, but we can provide various types of scaffolding to guide students' practice. Assignment sheets often include suggestions for how to approach a particular paper or offer grading criteria. Handouts and small-group prompts serve as scaffolding for in-class work. I also use simple conceptual models that help students remember complex ideas, such as a five-pointed, hand-drawn star that I often use to remind students of the various social institutions that shape culture (family, religion, government, education, and business), or a text analysis rubric that suggests five ways of approaching a text (content, structure, context, purpose, and reader). These and other scaffolding tools provide concrete guidance as students practice literary thinking.

Scaffolding allows me to do several things. First, an effective scaffold asks students to focus on a specific aspect of a text and to do so productively. Second and more important, scaffolding provides information and suggestions that encourage students to work in particular ways. Finally, some types of scaffolding can help students make concepts and strategies their own; through guided practice, they learn literary thinking strategies well enough to use them independently, without prompting or guidance.

One of my favorite examples is the style sheet. I find that students often have difficulty analyzing the style of a text. They come up with wonderful atmospheric descriptions, which reflect their experiences of reading the text, but they struggle to identify the qualities of the text that create that experience, the elements of its style. To my dismay, this is sometimes as true of students in my senior seminar as it is of those in my first-year writing classes. The difference is that once I remind the seniors of some element of style, they can discuss it easily, while the freshmen usually struggle with the very concept. But I think that senior English majors should pay attention to point of view, tone, sentence structure, and other aspects of literary style without prompting. I want them to internalize this vocabulary, to acquire the habit of considering multiple elements of style when they want to describe how a text works or what it is like.

By the time a student has completed an introductory-level literature course, they have probably heard several lectures and participated in some class discussions about style. In an upper-division literature course, students are not starting from scratch, but they still need practice. In advanced courses, practice may focus on delineating the styles of two movements, such as realism and modernism, or style may be used as a tool for comparing the work of two authors. In other words, we use style in intentional, focused ways. But in my experience, we can't have a high-quality discussion of style unless students can talk about it with some precision. And while I could certainly direct their attention to the style elements that I think matter, that would leave them dependent on my ability to analyze style rather than helping them develop their own skills.

I scaffold discussions about style by using a handout that lists a number of stylistic elements (see Table 1). The handout is always evolving and changing, based on the course in which I'm using it. The sheet gives students a brief version of what they might find in much more detail in a handbook on literary study, and it can seem simplistic. It's all pretty basic stuff, exactly the kind of thing we'd like to think that students have learned by the time they get to a specialized course on twentieth-century poetry or eighteenth-century novels. Indeed, I based mine on an example I found online, which was created by a high school English teacher.[3] The handout gives students a vocabulary for discussing style, and it serves as a checklist to remind them to consider multiple elements of style.

By itself, the handout serves as a model. It becomes the basis for scaffolding as we employ it in class discussions, using the list of style elements to guide discussions of poems and stories. After passing out the style sheet and quickly reviewing it, I ask students to work individually or in small groups to identify how one or two style elements function in a particular text. As a class, we discuss several elements, noting how they work together and any tensions that arise when style elements work differently. Often, we will devote a whole section of a course to working with style, using it as a tool to explore multiple texts and broad questions. In some classes, I have asked students to work in groups to plan a class session or presentation on how the style of an assigned

Table 1. Elements of Literary Style

Point of view	Through whose eyes do we see? Whose voice(s) are we hearing? Whose thoughts do we hear?
	Does the narrator tell you what people are thinking, or only what they do? Does the narrator comment on people's behavior, thoughts, or feelings?
	Is there more than one narrator or voice?
Sentence structure	Are the sentences long or short?
	How are the sentences structured—short and direct, or with multiple clauses and interjected phrases? Does the author use sentence fragments?
Pace	Do things happen quickly, or does the writer take a lot of time to describe the scene? Is the focus on events, descriptions, or thoughts?
Vocabulary	Are the words simple or fancy? Are they technical, flowery, colloquial, academic, slangy, obscure?
Tone	What is the narrator's attitude?
	What is the mood of the story?
	How does the author communicate mood and attitude?
Sound	Does the language create any noticeable sound effects—strong rhythm or rhyme, repeating sounds, sounds that imitate animals or music?
	How musical or rhythmic is the text? How does the writer achieve such effects?
Experimentation	Does the writer use any kind of unusual style—stream-of-consciousness, unusual layout on the page, breaking rules of grammar, shifting perspectives, and so on?
Figures of speech	Does the writer use metaphors, similes, or symbols?
	Do any words or phrases have multiple meanings?
Allusions	How does the author use references to other texts, myths, symbols, people, historical events, quotations, and so on?

Table 1. Elements of Literary Style (continued)

Dialogue	How much of the story/poem takes the form of dialogue?
	Do we hear whole conversations or just fragments?
	Does the conversation use informal style and slang, or is it more formal? Does it feel natural or contrived?
Structure	Are paragraphs or stanzas short or long? Or do they vary?
	Does the writer use a recognizable form, such as the sonnet or quatrains or a repeating rhyme scheme?
Sequencing	How has the author organized the text as a whole? How does the text move through time?
Metafictional techniques	Does the author call attention to or comment on his or her own narration?

Source: Adapted from Erik Christensen, Lakeside School. Used by permission.

reading relates to its ideas. In other classes, we use style as a pathway into conversations about themes and genres. For example, in my turn-of-the-twentieth-century American literature course, students often find Henry James's writing difficult. Their initial observations focus on how hard his work is, how it moves slowly and seems boring. Beyond complaining, though, they have difficulty articulating either his literary techniques or how they contribute to the meaning of his work. When students use the style sheet to compare James's writing in "The Real Thing" with that of Mary Wilkins Freeman in her short story "The New England Nun," they notice how point of view shapes each writer's use of description. Lisa, for example, pointed out that Freeman's description is "factual," presenting "physical details" that "paint an extremely vivid picture," while the descriptions in the James story clearly reflect the perspective of the character in whose voice the story is presented. As Amy noted in her discussion post about the two stories, this technique allows James to "intentionally distort the reader's perception." The style sheet gave these students a tool for analyzing the two writers' choices, and that allowed them to move beyond their initial gut responses to a more critical way of reading. At our next class meeting, we built on these informal analyses as we explored how the two stories reflect different ideas about the nature of art, reality, and the individual self. In the process, we developed our continuing discussion about the differences between realism and modernism. In other words, scaffolding students' analysis of style—reminding them to look at seemingly simple elements like point of view and word choice—prepared them for sophisticated conversations about patterns that reflected the broader historical issues at the heart of the course. Scaffolding strategic thinking is thus not an end in itself but a way of advancing students' engagement with content knowledge and complex literary analysis.

Constructing a Literary Toolbox

Working with the style sheet helps students develop their vocabulary for describing how literary texts work, and the handout serves as a prompt to remind them to consider aspects of a text that they might otherwise ignore. That's one of the major purposes of scaffolding. But scaffolding can also help students to develop awareness of the critical moves they already use and the stances they already take. When scaffolding emerges from students' work with texts, rather than prescribing how they will approach a text, the framework can help them recognize and value their prior learning and their abilities as literary critics. It's also important to remember that as useful as modeling and scaffolding can be, they work best as part of a sequence of activities that undergird ongoing class discussions and student assignments. I discovered this when I used a think-aloud to help students recognize, experiment with, and reflect critically on a concrete set of strategies for analyzing a text.

I began by trying to make my own thinking process visible by articulating my thoughts as I worked with a question about a literary text. Of course, on some level we are always making our thinking visible in the classroom. When I explain the relationship between the social issues related to urban life at the end of the nineteenth century and Sister Carrie's adventures in Chicago and New York, I am, after all, showing my thinking. But in most cases, what I'm revealing is an already-developed argument, and, as Wineburg says, presenting an argument "discloses few clues about the crucial decision points that allow sophis-ticated reasoning to emerge" (2001 91). He advocates showing students the messier thinking that we go through before we reach conclusions. Describing what we do requires us to pay attention to cognitive moves that are as invisible and unexamined to us as driving a car. I am an experienced driver, and I don't even think about the steps involved in starting my car and pulling out of my driveway every morning. I just do it, the same way I just read a story. Saying what we're thinking can feel awkward, but it can help students recognize the multifaceted, tentative, developmental process of literary interpretation.

I tried my first in-class think-aloud as an effort to remind students that the seemingly intuitive, magical process of figuring out how to begin interpreting a text actually involves some fairly clear and specific analytical strategies. I had been frustrated by students' uncertainty about developing their individual research projects in my American literature courses. When I suggested that they could use some of the strategies we were using in our discussions or some approaches they'd learned in other courses, they seemed stumped. They hadn't thought about what happened in class discussions as transferable strategies that they could apply to new situations. Instead, they seemed to assume that whatever I asked them to focus on as we looked at a novel or story was simply *the* way to read that text. They didn't realize that I was making choices about how to approach each text, nor did they see themselves as having access to a range of interpretive tools. They needed to see that *every* time we engage with a text, we make critical choices, and they needed to be reminded of the critical tools they already knew how to use.

In an effort to make these things visible, I vocalized my own thoughts when presented with a new question about a familiar text. I had asked students to come to class with questions about Charles Chesnutt's novel *The House behind the Cedars*. In class, students selected the question that they most wanted us to discuss, which was about the relationship between the two siblings in the story. I explained to the students that I was going to talk for ten to fifteen minutes, responding to this question, and I emphasized that the point of my demonstration was not to come up with an answer but to give them a chance to see how I wrestled with critical questions. I asked them to pay attention to and take notes about how I approached their question. What did I focus on? What kinds of questions and hypotheses did I pose? What intellectual moves and shifts did I make? I then did my best to think out loud. It felt strange, but students found it interesting. I'll admit that my thinking was not entirely spontaneous. Because I wanted students to recognize that literary thinking involves considering multiple approaches and selecting the ones that seem most productive, I deliberately took different approaches, and I highlighted ones that fit our course's emphasis on studying literature in historical perspective. I began by talking about the structure of the novel, how the narrator focuses first on one of the siblings and then on the other. I looked at specific passages in the text, commenting on whatever I noticed. As I continued, I talked about how this novel was similar to and different from others we'd read; about how the different social positions of the siblings reflected historical patterns about race, gender, and status; about how this novel follows some of the conventions of the "tragic mulatto" tale; and so on. My impromptu, improvisational riff on my students' question did not develop into a coherent argument about the novel. Instead, I deliberately showed students that I could approach a single question in a number of different ways.

But this demonstration was just the starting point. To make the concept concrete, I asked students to report on what they had noticed and how they thought my different approaches worked. Which seemed like the most useful avenues? How did the different approaches connect? What possibilities did I set aside? As students offered their observations, I took notes on the board, and before the next class period, I translated those notes into a list, "Strategies for Diving Deep," a phrase I often use to encourage students to make their interpretations more complex (see Table 2). The list included several possibilities, such as "chase the question through the text" (by identifying and discussing various passages that relate to the question), "speculate about the author's purpose," and "make comparisons and connections" (by looking for ways that the text relates to others from the period, the course, or the author). I also included some metacognitive strategies, like "rephrase the question," because I wanted to remind students to be self-aware and flexible. As I told my class, there probably wasn't anything on the list that they hadn't done before, or at least heard one of their professors do. Instead of listing new options, we had simply given names to a number of common strategies. That made them visible, and having a list of strategies reminded students that they had many tools available when they analyzed literary texts.

Because I wanted students to learn to think deliberately about which tools to use as they worked with literary problems, I asked them to work with this list in several ways. First, they worked in small groups, using different strategies to answer another question about the Chesnutt novel. After working for fifteen minutes or so, they presented their ideas, and we discussed what they had come up with. We used the strategies again in discussing the next text, Charlotte Perkins Gilman's *The Yellow Wallpaper*. Finally, to help students sharpen their ability to evaluate and monitor their own thinking, I asked them to post notes in an online discussion reflecting on which of the strategies they found most comfortable and most productive.

Students' responses suggest that the exercise made them conscious of their own habits and encouraged them to try out different strategies. Hillary wrote:

> I think in my own reading considering both context and how [a text] compares to other texts helps the most. I'm not going to focus on this, however, because they are familiar strategies to me, considerations I had already made before coming to class. I think the one strategy that most enlightened me over the past week is trying to define the author's purpose. Reason? Because it's a step I don't often take.

They began to recognize that the different strategies gave them multiple options, and that different strategies work well for different questions and texts. Laura explained in her post that she found the strategy of looking at different passages in the text most helpful in working with *The House behind the Cedars*, but that considering the author's biography helped her understand Gilman's story. Even more important, working with the strategies helped students become more aware of how their own thinking develops as they work with a text. Amy highlighted this in her description of what happened when her group reframed the question:

> When our group re-phrased the question, we came to the new question of "How do roles and identity affect the development of the plot and how we read the text?" This question encompasses

Table 2. Strategies for Diving Deep

Chase the question through the text.

- Consider the meaning/significance of specific words, phrases, descriptions, moments.
- Examine the characters—how they change, multiple examples of similar behavior, relationships.
- Identify key moments or developments in the plot—at what points do things change, and why? How do those changes relate to larger themes or tensions? How does a specific plot element shape what happens later?

Consider how the text reflects and was shaped by its context.

- Facts: information on publication, specific historical elements, or patterns. Is the text's depiction of X accurate?
- Issues: what did the public discussion of these themes look like? What tensions and debates were going on? What social changes were creating concerns, and what was the content of those concerns?
- Author's biography: what was this author's relationship with the issues in this text? How might that relationship have shaped the text?

Try to define the author's purpose.

- Ask questions about the function of specific choices—why did the author choose to make this character be this way? How does the author's style affect the text?
- Ask questions about the author's views about the themes of the text— what do we know about how s/he thought that could provide insight into the text? And what does the text tell us about how s/he thought?

Consider the audience(s)—past and present.

- Who were the original readers of this text? Were there multiple audiences? How might they have responded? What might the author have wanted to say to those different audiences?
- What do you bring to the text—knowledge, assumptions, attitudes, experiences—and how might that shape your focus, limit what you see, give you special insights?

Compare this text with others like it.

- How does this text represent patterns among similar texts? How does it violate those patterns?
- What do you know from other things you've read that can help you make sense of this text?

Table 2. Strategies for Diving Deep (continued)

Rephrase the original question.

- Expand it to encompass larger issues or to address a larger pattern in the text.
- Narrow it to focus on a specific case.
- Shift it to emphasize a slightly different aspect of the question or a related topic.

Defer reaching a conclusion—dive deeper.

- Offer hypotheses that you're not sure are correct, and explore them to see if they lead to new insights.
- Set ideas aside to return to later.
- Reject ideas that you believe are not working.
- Keep going even once you think you have a pretty good answer; find more possibilities, examples, reasons to develop your analysis.

ideas of why she went mad and introduces discussion of the husband/doctor roles and the narrator's loss of identity and role as a mother and wife. Like I said in my previous posting, our re-phrase got us going through the other strategies because there was a new focus. It was like a circle in a way. By re-phrasing we noticed a much larger pattern in the text.

As the course continued, and especially as students wrote outlines and drafts of their research papers, I referred to the list of strategies in my comments, encouraging them to consider different approaches to develop and complicate their analyses. Indeed, the list provided both my students and me with a kind of shorthand, so I could offer useful advice without lengthy explanation.

I've used this approach in subsequent classes, sometimes by making a list of strategies, sometimes by listing qualities of a genre or types of questions or some other set of ideas. I find that lists and other written models work best when we have generated them as a class. Working from their observations of a think-aloud or a class discussion makes the list feel organic rather than imposed. Because they have seen a strategy or concept at work, they know what to look for and what to expect, and they are more able to use it themselves. Our lists don't always use standard literary vocabulary, but that provides an opportunity for me to show students that they may already understand literary terms and concepts intuitively. They simply need to learn the right language and be more aware that they can draw on an array of strategies.

Scaffolding: Developing a Cognitive Apprenticeship Plan

Thinking about our teaching in terms of modeling and scaffolding requires a slight shift in how we plan courses, class meetings, and assignments. In the next few pages, I suggest some strategies to guide you through the development of your own cognitive apprenticeship plan, much as I might scaffold an assignment for students. As with any scaffold, the sections below provide reminders and suggestions, not requirements or firm rules. In other words, they will be most useful if you adapt them to suit your own needs and situation.

Articulating What Students Need to Learn

I usually begin planning both courses and class sessions by taking some time to think critically and selectively about the content and strategic knowledge I want students to learn. That may sound obvious, but as Showalter notes in *Teaching Literature,* we often plan literature courses around what we want students to read rather than around the concepts and strategies we want students to learn. Describing the content of a course in terms of learning feels awkward for many English professors, perhaps because we don't always separate ideas from texts. A particular text represents a set of ideas, so "covering" that text implies addressing those ideas. Certainly, that's how it was for me for the first fifteen years of my teaching career. No one ever asked me to write goals, and I remember being completely flummoxed by the task the first few times I had to do it. At first, I could only think of coverage goals: *students will become familiar with the literature of the mid-nineteenth century.* That statement translates into a very modest intention: we will read texts from that period. But, of course, I want students to read that material for a reason, and I hope that they will come away with literary knowledge that transcends the period we're studying. I want students to leave my courses with durable, flexible knowledge that they can apply to other courses, to other literary genres and periods, and even to the world around them. "Becoming familiar" doesn't fully capture that. Students need to understand how literature works and become adept at using a variety of tools for literary study. That analysis helped me draft goals that focus more on strategy and that are less specific to the period or theme of a course: *students will be able to locate, select, and use contextual knowledge to analyze literary texts; or, students will be able to identify connections and influences among writers of the period*. Getting to the point where I could articulate more substantive goals took a lot of time and experimentation. This isn't a way of thinking that comes naturally to most literature faculty. I hope you will try it anyway.

You can do this for a whole course, if you're at the stage of planning next semester's classes, or you can do it for the course you're teaching right now, just by thinking about what you want students to learn during the next week or two. Start with content knowledge, because that's the most familiar. But before you begin, consider this: in the long run, students are unlikely to remember the details. So instead of focusing on what you want students to learn about a specific text, consider the big ideas that you hope they will remember five years from now. In the broader landscape of literary studies, what significant issues and ideas are represented by this particular text or set of texts? The details help clarify the big ideas, so they will necessarily be part of the class, but they should not be the sole focus. Think big. For example, in my senior seminar Literature as Political Discourse, we spend plenty of time comparing how Carolyn Forché, Tony Kushner, and John Steinbeck use unexpected dramatic effects to create emotional responses in readers, but what I expect students to remember from those discussions is not the details of those texts but rather the idea that graphic imagery is both aesthetically interesting and a powerful rhetorical strategy. Stopping to articulate for myself the underlying ideas in a course or a single class session reminds me to make sure that those concepts emerge clearly in our class discussions.

I make a point of listing both content and strategic knowledge, if only to remind myself to pay attention to both as I plan the course, prepare a class session, or develop activities and assignments. That often means thinking critically about how I developed my own understanding of the texts and issues we're studying. It also means making choices about which part of my own process I want to emphasize. As I learned in the Jenny Lind research exhibit, trying to explain all of the elements of expert literary thinking at once just overwhelms and confuses students. In any course, on any class day, I have to make critical choices about what strategic knowledge best complements the content knowledge. So if we're talking about how Forché uses surprise and drama in her poem "The Colonel," I might pay more attention to helping students learn to notice and use poetic style and form than I would to making connections between historical context and the literary text. But if I wanted to focus our content knowledge about how literature reflects and comments on political events, I might emphasize strategic knowledge about thinking contextually and being aware of what we bring to the text, especially since most of my students know nothing about Latin American politics during the 1970s, when the poem was written. When I include these issues as I plan classes, I remember to draw students' attention to them in our discussions.

At first, thinking about your courses or class meetings this way might feel like an unnecessary extra step. None of us, after all, goes into class without having thought about what we want to accomplish that day. Too often, though, our thinking emphasizes coverage: I want to talk about the form of the sonnet, or I want to discuss feminist commentaries on Ophelia. Sometimes our thinking emphasizes engagement: how can I get them talking about this poem or story? Stopping to ask *why* we want to do that, considering the larger lessons that a specific approach teaches, makes us more mindful and can help us communicate more clearly not only what we want to cover but also why it matters. And with practice, this kind of mindfulness becomes habitual.

A good place to begin developing models and scaffolds is with the concepts or strategies that most trouble your students. Learning experts call these "bottlenecks."[4] What ideas do students find most confusing? In class discussions and student papers, what aspects of texts or elements of literary arguments do they use least effectively? It's helpful to work with modest and specific bottlenecks, rather than attempt to

"habitual mindfulness"

clarify a large and complex process all at once, as the Jenny Lind case taught me. Students have difficulty with many parts of research, but a written model of the whole process doesn't help them much. Instead, they need to learn specific strategies: how to work with critical articles, how to develop the questions that guide literary research, and how to develop an argument. No doubt, you have your own list of difficulties that trip up students semester after semester.

Once you've identified a bottleneck, try to determine why students have difficulty with that critical task. As I will discuss in chapter 4, looking closely at students' work may help you determine the source of their difficulties, while thinking critically about your own work can help you identify your own strategies. Recognizing the difference between how you approach a critical task and how your students do it can clarify the nature of a bottleneck. Once you know which concepts, information, skills, or habits of mind your students need to learn, you can begin to develop relevant models and scaffolds.

Let me share an example by using a common bottleneck: students' research habits. When I read students' papers, it often seems as if they grabbed the first five articles or books they found and plopped in a few almost random quotes just to fulfill the requirement that they use outside research. They rarely engage thoughtfully with helpful or relevant ideas from critical articles or primary cultural sources. At first, I speculated that the problem was that students simply weren't taking the time to think about what they were looking for, so I asked them to create research plans at least a month before the paper was due. That didn't help much, because most of their plans were so vague. Students wrote that they needed articles and books, which was accurate but wouldn't help them conduct research strategically. As we talked about their approach to research, I realized that they didn't understand the different types of sources available, nor did they know how to choose the most useful sources and use them well. I also thought about the knowledge I bring to planning my own research: in addition to having a sophisticated understanding of how to use online research databases, I also understand what types of information different kinds of sources provide. I recognize fairly easily whether a particular article or book will be useful. The latter results from years of experience, and I can't easily teach that, but I can help students understand the different types of sources available. I created a handout listing several major types of literary sources, where to find each type, and what kinds of information each might provide (see Table 3). I also talked in class about my own current research and how I had determined what type of sources I needed. I had identified the bottleneck, diagnosed its cause, modeled my own research process, and developed a written model that could serve as a scaffold as students began their research. Sure enough, armed with that table, students were able to develop more specific research plans and locate more appropriate sources. Before I could model and scaffold the research process effectively, though, I had to define what I wanted students to know, what difficulties they encountered, and the knowledge and habits that I drew upon in my own research.

Showing Your Work

Lists, tables, charts, and other written models or summaries of key literary ideas can function as both models and scaffolds. I also like to use conceptual analogies, as in the music video exercise or the five-pointed star. Analogies function as mnemonics to help students remember core ideas and, when they work well, to clarify the relationships among core ideas. Such tools help students use abstract concepts, because they make them easier to remember and provide a guide to using such concepts. If students hold the image of a cube in their heads, for example, they may be more likely to remember to consider multiple aspects of the text—author, context, audience, form, style, story. In order for an analogy or written model to work well, it must fit comfortably with the concept you're illustrating, and it must be accessible enough that students will easily connect the unfamiliar concept with the familiar analogy or outline.

Sometimes I provide a model, like the style sheet, and sometimes we develop it together as part of a class activity or discussion. For example, whenever I teach a course that is defined historically, such as a survey or period course, I begin by asking students to construct a timeline reflecting what they know about the relevant literary and cultural history. For my course on the 1950s, we focus on the twentieth century, but for a survey, I might ask students to construct a timeline of the entire history of American literature. The timeline exercise gives me some

Table 3. Sources for Literary Research

If You Want to Know . . .	Primary Sources	Secondary Sources
How people viewed a particular issue during a period of history	nonfiction writing about the subject ■ magazine articles ■ newspaper articles ■ pamphlets ■ books fiction that addresses the subject popular culture about the subject ■ popular songs ■ advertisements ■ images private writings, such as diaries and letters	historical studies about the period historical studies about the issue studies of the writer (or of literature in general) that focus on that issue critical articles about your book that focus on this issue
The writer's view of the issue and/or this text	other published writings by this person, including essays about literature and pieces of fiction letters and diaries biographical reports from the period about the issue or the text	biographies of the writer studies of the writer's work critical articles that focus on the writer's perspective
How people responded to the text	reviews published at the time articles about the author published during that period or soon thereafter letters and diaries (though these are very hard to find)	critical articles that focus on readers' responses biographies of the writer studies of the writer's career

Table 3. Sources for Literary Research (continued)

If You Want to Know . . .	Primary Sources	Secondary Sources
How this book compares with others from the period or by the writer	other works published at the time reviews published at the time of this and similar books essays about literature published at the time	studies of the writer's career (both individual articles and books) studies of the genre or movement (both individual articles and books)

sense of students' prior knowledge and their assumptions about literary history. At the same time, it reminds students of what they already know. Students often begin by insisting that they don't know anything about literary history, but as they fill in the timeline, they realize that they really do bring significant knowledge to the course. The exercise also reminds them to use what they've learned in other courses, and it reinforces the idea that no historical period is isolated from the rest of literary and cultural history. The timeline makes visible and concrete an underlying theme of literature surveys and of courses that focus on specific periods: literature is historically situated. That's not news to most students, but the timeline exercise takes a fairly abstract, vague concept and makes it concrete and specific.

Most of the ideas that we would put on a list or in a table exist somewhere else in another form. Literary terms are explained in literature handbooks, and the major influences and patterns of literary history are summarized in the introductory notes to sections of anthologies. Other ideas that we would put in a written model might be introduced as part of a background lecture or class discussion. The problem is that students either don't read, don't understand, or don't remember these sources, and many take minimal or poor notes in class. Creating written "cheat sheets" may seem to coddle students, and some might say that it's condescending to assume that students won't learn the material without this kind of aid. Shouldn't we assume that students are capable of recognizing, understanding, and remembering these things without such conceptual crutches? Can't we count on them to use the information that's available in handbooks and anthologies? In an ideal universe, yes. In my classroom experience, this rarely occurs. By synthesizing the most relevant and useful material in a one- or two-page handout, we make the information easy for students to remember and use. By integrating the information on those handouts into lectures, class discussions, and assignments, we encourage students to practice and eventually to internalize literary knowledge and strategies.

One of the most basic forms of modeling involves deliberately drawing students' attention to the underlying concepts and processes you're using in class. You can do this in several ways. A simple version is framing. By introducing the concepts and strategies that will come into play in each class session, you can draw students' attention to the big issues that frame whatever specific texts or questions you're exploring. For example, early in a course on the American novel, I suggested a process-oriented frame, listing some key elements of the analytical process: observant reading, posing questions, hypothesizing, contextualizing, identifying evidence, and mapping an argument. As we moved through the first few novels, we also moved through this process. Our discussions of *Huck Finn* focused on observant reading and questioning. With *Uncle Tom's Cabin,* we focused on moving from questions to hypothesizing answers. By the time we reached Willa Cather, we were ready to focus on how evidence could support an analysis. This kind of framing can help students understand how a specific class session fits into the course as a whole. In many literature courses, the goals listed on the syllabus disappear from view after the first day of class. For the instructor, those goals may still shape what happens in class, but students don't necessarily recognize that. Drawing attention to how today's discussion relates to the larger goals can reinforce students' learning, both because it makes the purpose of today's class clear and because it reminds students that we are studying a specific text or issue in order to gain understanding of a larger concept.

Another approach involves commenting on your own thought processes during a lecture or discussion. This can draw students' attention to how you are using the course concepts and to the thinking processes you used to develop your reading of a text or the questions you're posing to shape class discussion. The idea is to make visible both the fact that you are making choices and the ideas, theories, background knowledge, questions, assumptions, and habits that influence those choices. This makes modeling sound exhausting, but it can be relatively easy. When you tell students why you're approaching a text in a certain way, you're modeling. Modeling can also involve noting the background information that focuses your attention or informs your reading. Instead of just telling students about the social issues that influenced a particular text, you might explain how you know that those social issues matter, or how you learned about those issues. Following Gerald Graff's call for us to "teach the conflicts," modeling might lead us to simply acknowledge that we have chosen a particular way of approaching a text and that other approaches exist. Better yet, we might explain why we chose this one. In doing so, we demonstrate that our critical reading strategies are neither wholly idiosyncratic—*that's just the way Sherry thinks*—nor in any way "natural" to the text—*that's the right way to read this novel*.

A more deliberate and less natural way of modeling is the think-aloud I described above, a demonstration of expert thinking in process. This might involve literally thinking out loud about a specific literary problem or text, but you can achieve a similar outcome by preparing a description of the thinking process outside of class and sharing it with students in retrospect. This can help students understand that literary analysis isn't magic, nor is it simple, and it can highlight and demystify strategies they can use to develop their own literary thinking.

Asking students to track the content and strategic knowledge we use can also function as a kind of modeling. As in the think-aloud exercise, I will often ask students to pay attention to the critical moves we make in a class discussion. Sometimes, I ask a few people to take on the roles of observer and recorder, and their notes help the class reflect on what strategies we used and how well we used them. This process fosters habits of metacognition and reflection. I like this approach because it encourages students to think on multiple levels—to discuss the text or issue while also being aware of the choices they are making, the knowledge they bring to bear on the discussion, and the strategies they are using. I also want them to develop the habit of noticing how their professors, their peers, and they themselves think and speak about literature. If, as I noted in chapter 1, much of our teaching of literature communicates underlying concepts and strategies indirectly, between the lines, then I want students to become critical readers of literature class discussions and lectures in the same way I want them to become critical readers of literary texts. Asking them to notice and evaluate what happens in class can help them develop that awareness.

Facilitating Good Practice

Models work best when they are integrated into the course and translated into practice. In other words, if you want students to remember what you model, give them the opportunity to practice using it. Regardless of the form in which we present them, ideas or information remain relatively useless until students understand how they function as tools for literary interpretation and analysis. This is one of the reasons that I'm partial to written models and conceptual analogies: they give students portable and concrete tools that they can begin using fairly easily. The best way to ensure that students understand the concepts and develop the ability to use literary knowledge is for them to apply the ideas in class and on their own. As I described earlier with the "Strategies for Diving Deep" example, I like to give students multiple opportunities to use and reflect on critical practices. This can happen in a full-class discussion, using questions that guide students to apply ideas from a written model. Full-class discussions rarely give everyone the opportunity to practice, though, so I also ask students to practice in small groups. Small-group discussions work best with clear, concrete prompts, and written models facilitate this. Each group can be assigned to wrestle with a specific part of the model, and the whole class can join in a discussion as groups present their conclusions.

Neither full-class discussions nor small groups ensure that every student will practice using the concepts or strategies. In every class, there are always a few students who are quite adept at sitting back and observing or, worse, just being in the room without engaging at all. To reach everyone, I use individual informal writing assignments, which provide additional practice even for those who have been active in class.

An online discussion board works well for this, as do in-class writing assignments and journals. By asking every student to work with each strategy several times over the course of the semester, I build practice into the course, and that helps students begin to internalize expert literary thinking practices. Because students are not yet adept at applying what they're learning, they need opportunities for low-stakes practice—small assignments that don't count for a significant portion of their course grade. Worrying about getting things right creates anxiety and can often narrow students' thinking. I want them to play with what they're learning, to become comfortable with it. Short, informal writing tasks don't take significant amounts of time for students to prepare or for me to review.

Students learn to use a strategy best through repetition. Using a written model to frame an introductory lecture and then using the model as a scaffold in class discussion, small-group conversations, and individual writing ensures that students hear about and then use ideas and strategies multiple times. On first glance, it might seem that this would become tiresome, but in practice, this kind of scaffolding creates coherence. Applying the same concepts or reading practices to a series of texts helps weave different parts of the course together. Repetition reinforces students' learning, and variation helps them develop the ability to apply a set of ideas or a literary thinking strategy to new material and different situations. The process also helps students recognize that they have an extensive set of tools for literary analysis, and it helps them develop the ability to select the right tool for a given problem and to use it well.

Metacognition Matters

If students are learning reasonably well how to use literary thinking strategies, why does it matter if they can't identify what they're doing? Isn't the ability to do it what matters most? It may seem ironic, since expertise involves the internalization and naturalization of ways of thinking, but expertise also relies on metacognition. While literary thinking feels creative and intuitive, our expertise also involves the ability to recognize and evaluate our own thinking. Metacognition may be even more important for our students. Part of what distinguishes experts from novices is the ability to determine a useful strategy for dealing with a new problem, evaluate how well a strategy is working, and try a different approach. What students learn in our courses provides them with resources from which they can select, intentionally and thoughtfully, as they move on to additional courses, their own research, the workplace, and their lives.

By making thinking visible and providing students with opportunities to refine their literary thinking strategies, modeling and scaffolding help them develop adaptive expertise. If students are to develop fully their abilities as literary thinkers, they need to see what literary thinking looks like. They must recognize that the ability to read and interpret well isn't a mystical gift or a talent magically conferred upon professors, but the result of using various skills and strategies. But observation is not enough. Students also need opportunities to practice, with guidance, to apply their knowledge effectively. As my childhood piano teacher used to tell me, practice makes permanent, not necessarily perfect. Scaffolding can help students practice well. At the same time, students need to develop their ability to evaluate and adapt their own practice. Because modeling and scaffolding give names and methodological clarity to aspects of literary thinking that feel implicit and intuitive, they help students not only become better literary thinkers but also become aware of their own developing expertise. We can build modeling and scaffolding into our teaching in relatively simple, modest ways, without having to rethink entire courses or curricula. That said, I also believe that courses that are designed to build students' abilities over the term, through incremental, recursive practice and with regular coaching from faculty, can work even better to help students become better literary thinkers. In chapter 3, I'll suggest an approach to course design that applies these ideas on the level of the whole course.

3 ■ Course Design for Literary Learning

In *Teaching Literature,* Elaine Showalter suggests that most English faculty begin course planning by making a list of readings, figuring out how much time to devote to each, and determining the best order for working with these texts. Of course, this isn't a merely technical process. Implicit in our decisions about readings and schedules are ideas about how the knowledge of the discipline is structured. This seemingly minimalist, practical process reflects deep knowledge of our discipline. Still, course design usually emphasizes content knowledge— what we want students to understand about literature, rather than what we want them to be able to do with literature. Although many course syllabi include strategic knowledge goals, such as "strengthen students' ability to read and think critically" or "develop the ability to present literary arguments," we usually plan courses around what content to cover. Neither our reading selections nor our course plans reflect significant attention to *how* students will develop their literary thinking.

Such attention doesn't always shape our writing assignments either. Ideally, assignments should either help students develop their literary thinking and writing skills or allow them to demonstrate what they've learned, or both. Short essays, especially when students write several of them during the semester, and informal writing work well for both of these purposes. Unfortunately, the most common assignment in advanced literature courses, the end-of-term research paper, often doesn't achieve either goal. Our students would benefit from more strategic thinking on our part about what kinds of assignments will best facilitate their learning. They could also use more guidance about and support for the literary writing process. While our colleagues in composition have designed effective strategies for developing students' writing abilities, most literature faculty provide only minimal instruction in writing. Too often, we assume that students already know how to write about literature and how to do literary research, so we offer little guidance as they develop their papers, and even when we intend our comments as constructive criticism, students rarely get the chance to apply our suggestions. Their most ambitious work, the research paper, usually arrives at the end of the semester, after all, and students may not pay much attention to comments at that point. At the end of the term, we're all ready to get on with other things.

Designing effective courses and assignments requires that we think purposefully and strategically about both what we want students to learn and how we think learning occurs. While habit, training, and disciplinary culture may lead us to focus almost entirely on covering content knowledge, we should also think about how to foster students' development of strategic knowledge. However, as John V. Knapp writes, determining how to help students learn isn't easy: "*how* to create bridges between expert and novice—other than assigning massive doses of unmotivated 'outside reading' or by giving lengthy and potentially often soporific lectures—remains one of the unresolved, persistent problems in college literature teaching today" (59). I don't pretend to have conclusive solutions to that problem. I do, however, believe that we can begin to build those bridges by shifting the focus of our teaching, including how we design courses, to emphasize learning and doing—the process of learning as well as the process of doing literary work.

How might that shift of emphasis change the way we plan courses? First, it would require us to think more deliberately about what we want students to learn, as well as about what experiences help students develop understanding and abilities. We might approach assignments more as developmental opportunities rather than seeing them primarily as summative performances of acquired knowledge. We might also rethink our own roles in the classroom and our responsibilities as coaches who can help students improve their work. All of this would, at least at first, take more time, if only because learning-centered course design is an unfamiliar way of approaching a task that we already know how to do reasonably well. Yet, not only can a more learning-centered, process-oriented approach improve our students' learning, it can also, ultimately, make teaching more rewarding.

Teachers in many fields have made this kind of shift since the turn of the twenty-first century, moving from content-centered to student-centered to learning-centered teaching. This involves a different theoretical and strategic approach to course design, but the result, as I will show, can improve students' learning. I don't offer my approach to teaching literature as *the* perfect model. This approach to course design can generate a wide range of models. Learning-centered teaching stems from three core practices: the use of a "backward design" method that begins with critical thinking about what students should learn and what "good learning" looks like, assignments that develop students' disciplinary thinking abilities incrementally, and strategies for providing significant, constructive feedback to help students improve their abilities. It all comes together in a course design tool that can help make a complex model both creative and manageable.

Backward Design

When I first encountered backward design, I scoffed at the idea that it could be useful to me. The concept was presented in a slim, workbook-like volume clearly aimed at K-12 teachers, and it seemed at first to define teaching and learning in rather simplistic ways. What could this elementary school model have to offer me? But as I started to play with the ideas presented by Grant Wiggins and Jay McTighe in *Understanding by Design,* I found that their approach could help me think more critically and clearly about what I wanted students to learn, how to facilitate their learning, and how they might demonstrate that they understood course concepts. The model can seem formulaic, but it frames some significant and challenging questions that have become, for me, essential tools for good teaching.

Wiggins and McTighe argue that we should not plan courses around the material we want to cover. Rather, they advocate building courses around "enduring understandings," big ideas that transcend a single course. We must still select which materials to cover, but in backward design, readings are chosen based on how well they will help students understand the big ideas. In backward design, readings and the course schedule are the final concerns, not the starting place. The model has taught me to begin course planning with three deceptively simple questions:

- What do I want students to understand at the end of this course?
- How could they effectively demonstrate that understanding?
- What experiences and information will help them develop that understanding and the ability to demonstrate it effectively?

Within each of these seemingly obvious questions are embedded several truly challenging problems. It's quite easy, for example, to say that I want students to understand the history of nineteenth-century American literature. But what does that mean, and why does it matter? What is the value of understanding that history in the broader context of the English major? What does it look like when someone understands nineteenth-century American literary history? And how do students acquire significant understanding of literary history?

Among the most challenging concepts in backward design is the idea that our courses should be built around Wiggins and McTighe's enduring understandings. We are used to writing course goals either that emphasize coverage ("examine a range of texts written in the seventeenth century") or that are shorthand for extremely complex, even contradictory ideas ("understand the history of nineteenth-century American literature"). Wiggins and McTighe suggest that we should instead build courses around core disciplinary concepts. They define *enduring understandings* as ideas that have relevance for the discipline at large, though they may also reflect concepts from specific subfields, theoretical schools, or approaches. Enduring understandings have significance beyond a single course. For example, the enduring understanding that literary texts have been shaped by and may in turn influence the culture in which they were created is as central to a course on Shakespeare as it is to a course on contemporary Latina poetry. Similarly, the enduring understanding that meaning resides both in a text, in its content, form, and style, *and* in the reader's active engagement with the text might provide a focus for any number of literature courses. Enduring understandings may also reflect strategic knowledge, such as the idea that literary arguments usually incorporate a combination of textual and contextual evidence, theoretical models, and awareness of the arguments made by previous critics. Courses should emphasize enduring understandings partially because they matter most. Understanding core concepts and strategies prepares students to apply their knowledge in new situations. It enables transfer and development, and it helps make the overall curriculum more coherent.

In a way, of course, that's what we already do. Even if we begin course planning by selecting readings, those choices rest on core ideas of our discipline. The ideas are present, but they are implicit. Wiggins and McTighe suggest that we should articulate the big ideas that we most want students to understand, because courses designed with such goals clearly in mind are more likely to achieve the kind of learning we want for our students. If we articulate the enduring understandings that are the goals of our courses, we may make better choices about what to read and what assignments to require, and we can more clearly communicate to students why the course matters. The significance of a course may be obvious to us, but we have a privileged relationship with the literature and theory we teach. Not only do we know it well, we have an investment in it. Not so for our students, and they may not even recognize that a course has an underlying theme or purpose. Some students will pick up on core concepts, but for many, literature courses seem like a loosely connected series of discussions of readings from the same period or genre. Almost none of the students I interviewed could identify a core theme or concept in any of their courses. Instead, they described them as being about the readings: English 207 is about twentieth-century British novels or English 305 is about Shakespeare. The enduring understandings of literary studies may seem self-evident to us, but they are often invisible to our students.

It is possible to revise typical literature course goals into statements of enduring understandings, but doing so can be challenging and even unsettling. Consider the example of my nineteenth-century literature course. When I say that I want students to understand the "history of nineteenth-century American literature," what I really mean is that I want them to understand how American literature developed in relation to ideas about the United States as a nation and a culture, in response to literary forms and styles that originated in England but changed as they moved through various regions and periods, in dialogue with the changing population and culture of a rapidly growing country, in tension with a wide variety of social and artistic conflicts, and much more. The "history of nineteenth-century American literature," it turns out, is such a large and undefined concept that it is almost unteachable. More important, a course goal that encompasses so much offers me almost no guidance other than the coverage model for planning a course, and it communicates almost nothing to my students about the core issues of the course.

In order to revise that goal into an enduring understanding, I have to consider how "understanding the history of nineteenth-century American literature" reflects core disciplinary concepts. In other words, I have to acknowledge that what matters about my course may not be the specific period or genre that it covers but the way the course illustrates a broader set of literary concerns. As Jerome Bruner suggests in *The Process of Education*, "To understand something as a specific instance of a more general case . . . is to have learned not only a specific thing but also a model for understanding other things like it that one may encounter" (qtd. in Wiggins and McTighe 12). So what is the "more general case" for which my nineteenth-century course is the "specific instance"? And what is the substance of that general case? Put differently, in order to clarify the enduring understandings of this course, I have to consider why literary studies puts so much emphasis on literary history.

In truth, we don't just want students to be merely *familiar* with a large number of authors, texts, and styles, though we do want them to know about (and ideally to have read) some especially significant texts and styles. We want them to be able to position an unfamiliar text in the appropriate literary and cultural history. Why? Because we believe that historical context—literary and social—provides keys to or, some would say, is the basis for the meaning and significance of a text. In order for students to interpret literature well, they need to understand how and why literature has changed. Students need to understand that literature has developed over time, as writers influence each other and are influenced by their cultures, and that paying attention to the relationship between history—both literary and social—and the text can help us read literature better. On the one hand, nineteenth-century American literature serves as a case study to help students learn an abstract concept that lies at the very heart of literary studies today. By studying nineteenth-century American literature, students will see how ideas about literary form and style, relationships among writers, and changing ideas and debates about American society contributed to the movement from sentimental and philosophical writing to more realist and regionalist literature. On the other hand, the specific literary history of this period also matters. If I want students to be able to interpret an unfamiliar nineteenth-century American text using its historical context, they need to know about the conditions, qualities, and elements (writers, texts, movements, forms) of that era in American literature. Notice how that sentence begins to narrow and define the content of the "history of nineteenth-century American literature." My course goal thus becomes two enduring understandings, one about why history matters in the study of literature and another about the conditions, qualities, and elements of the literature of a specific place and time.

These concepts may seem to be tightly focused on content knowledge, which seems to run counter to my emphasis on strategic knowledge. But in this example, the enduring understandings encompass both content and strategic knowledge. The concept of literary history may well emphasize content, but one part of my enduring understanding—"paying attention to the relationship between history and the text"—calls for strategic knowledge. Once students understand that history matters, they must develop the ability to acquire new information about literary and social history and make connections between history and texts. Strategic knowledge includes the ability to identify which aspects of nineteenth-century American literary history would be relevant to a particular text or question.

This observation points us to the second question of backward design: how can students demonstrate that they understand?

Demonstration suggests an ability to do something with knowledge, but it also challenges us to think about what it means to truly understand a literary concept, period, or genre. It is one thing for students to recognize and discuss the connections between industrialization, social reform, and Rebecca Harding Davis's *Life in the Iron Mills* when I provide the background material, identify major themes, and guide the discussion, but can they perform the same kind of analysis on another text, without my guidance? That, for me, would demonstrate real understanding. John Webster articulates the distinction nicely in his discussion of students' learning about Spenser in his British literature survey course: "I had certainly shown them what I was after, had modeled it, had worked through stanzas with them in class. But while they could follow that sort of discourse, and redact it at least partially if asked, their work showed that few of them could go on to new stanzas and cantos on their own" (198). Many of us share Webster's experience: we want to help students develop independent literary thinking abilities, but we know that we're not yet accomplishing that goal. That takes us to the third question: how do we help students develop understanding? What has to happen, in class or as students work on their own, to help them move from being able to follow literary discourse to being able to analyze texts on their own?

Webster's experience is instructive here, because it illustrates how focusing on what we want students to understand and how we define understanding can strengthen our teaching and enhance students' learning. Webster made two important shifts as he tried to solve the problem of students' persistent difficulties with Spenser. First, instead of asking himself "how much of *The Faerie Queene* should I cover, and how much time from a ten-week quarter should I take to do it?" (197), he tried to figure out how studying Spenser could help students develop their abilities as readers and critics of Spenser's poetry, something which could, in turn, help them read any kind of poetry. Second, he moved from demonstrating how to read Spenser to asking students to work with the text on their own, with his assistance and encouragement. In the "stanza workshop," students selected stanzas that seemed significant or interesting to them and then worked individually and in small groups to analyze them. This meant looking at only a few stanzas at a time, so students read less of the larger work than they would in a more traditional approach. The result, he claims, was improvement in students' ability to read and write about Spenser, as well as increased confidence and better understanding of this particular poem and of poetry in general. As Webster's example shows, we can improve students' learning of both content and strategic knowledge by focusing more on giving them opportunities to practice working with literary texts.

This model of performative understanding guides both how I design courses and my daily teaching practice. Students won't fully understand either content or strategic literary knowledge until they use it. Further, the ability to use ideas doesn't come from watching someone else use them. It comes from practice, from using them yourself. Webster's observation that modeling and guided discussion left students unable to read and analyze unfamiliar stanzas and cantos illustrates the difference. English majors should develop the ability to analyze literature independently, not merely repeat or imitate what their professors do. We can help students achieve that ability through course designs based on what we want students to understand, designs that provide ample opportunities for students to practice using those concepts.

The best course designs also provide opportunities for repeated practice and for movement from relatively simple tasks to more complex ones. Webster has students repeat the stanza workshop multiple times, for example, taking on larger chunks of text and developing more complex interpretations over the three weeks that he devotes to *The Faerie Queene.* This gives students opportunities for productive failure. Doing the same task multiple times reduces the pressure to get it right the first time and offers multiple opportunities for students to learn from their mistakes and our feedback. As Webster explains, his approach "keeps the stakes, and the risks, low and thus allows for mere good tries and even errors," experiences he argues that "novices need but are often not allowed" (201). Repetition also builds confidence, increases capability, and develops independence. As students do similar activities multiple times, the teacher can gradually step back, giving students more independence as they become more adept. In cognitive apprenticeship, this is called *fading,* and it's a crucial part of the process because it recognizes and encourages student growth and independence. Creating opportuni-

"fading"

ties for repeated practice has important implications for course structures. As Webster's case suggests, shifting the focus to learning by doing and repeated practice means that we must move more slowly through texts. We simply will not be able to get through as many pages of reading. But, he argues, the trade-off is more than worthwhile.

The three core questions of backward design highlight the primary decisions that we need to make in course design, and starting with defining what we want students to learn ensures that all of our design decisions contribute to that learning. Once I have a clear idea of what I really want students to learn, I can begin to think about what assignments will allow them to demonstrate their learning and what kinds of practice they need. Two additional concepts are helpful at this point. First, as cognitive research suggests, learning is not only developmental, in the sense that it occurs over time, but also *incremental*—new learning is always built on prior learning. This suggests that we should view assignments and learning experiences as part of a larger process and structure them incrementally, so that they build on each other as students develop expertise over the course of the semester. In addition, three key elements of cognitive apprenticeship guide my course design. First, students benefit from scaffolding that guides them as they use unfamiliar concepts and strategies. Second, individual and group coaching helps students refine their knowledge and skills. Feedback helps students recognize their strengths and weaknesses, and effective coaching includes suggestions for improvement. Finally, because students become more adept over time, they require less scaffolding and coaching later in the semester. All of this means that designing assignments is the most important part of my course design process.

Rethinking the Research Paper

So far, I've been discussing "learning by doing" primarily in terms of what we ask students to do in class, but of course students do a substantial portion of their literary thinking outside of class, as they read texts, prepare for exams, and write informal and formal assignments. Writing assignments and other projects are the most active and, I would argue, the most productive of these activities. Reading is the necessary starting place for literary study, and exams provide opportunities for students to demonstrate that they remember key points from lectures and discussions, but (as our composition colleagues have long argued) writing fosters, shapes, and captures students' thinking. Because writing can be a tool for figuring out what we think, as well as for finding a way to articulate developing ideas or hunches, informal writing is common in literature courses. In-class writing, online discussions, and journals prompt students to capture their initial thoughts and responses and begin to frame their ideas in preparation for discussion, and they also provide a space for reflection about what happens in class. More formal papers, such as response essays, short analyses, and research papers, ask students to articulate their ideas more carefully, which should also push them to take more time and think more critically.

Course design presents us with an opportunity to engage in our own critical thinking, not only about what we teach and how we conduct classes but also about how we use assignments. Traditionally, informal writing has served to help students develop ideas, while formal papers have provided opportunities for students to demonstrate their learning. While we might all agree that writing a short essay or a longer research paper provides learning opportunities, we don't always design these assignments in ways that deliberately foster and support learning. Assignment sheets may explain the purpose of the paper and provide suggestions for how to approach doing it, but we provide few opportunities for students to practice or improve the critical thinking, research, and academic writing that generate strong essays. We may offer advice for how to do better in comments on a finished paper, but unless students have the chance to either rewrite the paper or write another essay of the same kind, our suggestions have limited effect. Research papers, especially, usually arrive on our desks at the end of the term, too late for us to help students write better papers. No doubt, writing papers can facilitate students' learning while also showing us how well they're learning. Making that happen, however, may require us to think differently both about the assignments we design and about how they fit into our courses.

The gap between our teaching goals and how well our assignments either contribute to or demonstrate student learning is, I believe, most significant with the research paper. The research paper is the most common type of assignment in advanced literature courses: 78.3 percent of the faculty I surveyed assign them in most classes, and another 17.4 percent do so "sometimes." Why? One reason may be that the research paper involves students in the types of work that literary scholars do, albeit on a smaller scale and in a much shorter time frame. An argument supported by research represents the most sophisticated and substantive form of literary work, and that kind of analysis is what literary thinking looks like. "Doing literary work" means making arguments about texts based on analysis of the texts themselves, their contexts, and existing critical debates. The ubiquity of the research paper is not at all surprising, nor is it necessarily problematic.

Indeed, the research paper has much to offer as a culminating assignment for English majors. First, research paper assignments often give students flexibility in selecting a topic. Many lists of "best practices" in teaching make the claim that students learn best when they can pursue their own interests. When students choose or shape their research topics, they may be more likely to develop a sense of competence and investment in the discourse community of literary studies. Second, research papers often give students opportunities to apply what they're learning in the course to new material or to develop further an analysis begun in class. Writing a research paper requires students to practice and hone their abilities as researchers and writers. They must frame topics or questions; locate, select, and use sources; develop their own analyses; and present their arguments in appropriate and persuasive ways. Because these are core thinking skills in literary studies, students need to develop them, and the research paper creates opportunities for learning these important elements of strategic knowledge.

If only it worked. Haven't we all been disappointed and frustrated with the quality of students' research papers? Not only are many papers poorly developed and awkwardly written, often they don't show whether students have acquired an understanding of the core ideas of the course. My own investigation of the problem of the research paper began after an especially frustrating set of papers from my turn-of-the-twentieth-century American lit course. Although the course had emphasized the connections between the historical context, including social and artistic issues of the period, and the literary works, almost none of the students discussed historical context in their research papers. Instead, they wrote about plot and character; they suggested that the author's psychological makeup or life experience was being echoed in his or her writing (with a focus on things like whether the author had a happy childhood or a good marriage, not on how the author's perspective might have been influenced by the issues of the day); or they focused on themes without referencing context at all. Indeed, in some cases, the only connection between their papers and the course was that they examined texts written during the appropriate period. Students wrote about relevant topics and texts, but they rarely used ideas from the course in their analyses. And if the papers didn't demonstrate students' learning, then what was the point?

Some would argue that the point is not to use knowledge from the course but rather to develop the ability to think independently, to practice literary criticism. But the papers didn't seem to be accomplishing that either. Students' analyses were often thin, focusing on the surface level of what happens in a novel or story and revealing little in the way of complexity. They had an especially difficult time using outside sources well. They sprinkled quotes through their papers but rarely commented on, argued with, or built upon what the critics said, and almost no one used contextual sources. I was deeply discouraged, but I suspected that these problems were not occurring only in my classes. My hunch was confirmed by my department's assessment of papers from several sections of the senior seminar, which showed that few students were able to use primary and secondary sources well.

So we have a paradox. The research paper has great potential to help students both develop and demonstrate their literary thinking skills. In practice, it often fails to fulfill either of these purposes. Why? The problem rests in part on the habits and concepts students bring to our courses. As cognitive psychologists argue, prior learning shapes students' understanding in new courses.[1] Because their prior experience with college writing has taught students some misguided (and unintentional) lessons, most don't approach writing a research paper in thoughtful and productive ways. Unfortunately, we often contribute to these problems through poorly designed research paper assignments.

If we understand the misconceptions and obstacles that shape students' work, we can develop assignments that provide more structure and clearer guidance, and help students develop stronger analyses.

One of the most common mistakes students make is waiting to start the paper until late in the term. We often give the assignment early in the semester, because we know that developing an analysis takes time. We want to give students ample time to select a good topic, gather sources, and develop their ideas. But no matter how early in the semester we give term paper assignments, most students will complete them quickly, in a week or two at most, near the due date. Many students operate on a just-in-time model for all of their schoolwork. Yes, students are busy, and many believe that they work best under pressure, but they also don't know how to use the time we give them.

We try to help them. We encourage them to do their research carefully and thoughtfully, but they may not know what to look for, or even why reading critical articles or related primary materials would be valuable. We might remind them to use scholarly databases rather than Google, and we emphasize the importance of citing sources properly. But we don't say much about how research helps us develop a better analysis. As students' papers often demonstrate, many are unsure about how to use ideas and information outside of the text itself. This may be especially true of primary sources. Students don't know how to locate or use historical materials effectively. We model the use of contextual sources, drawing on our own thorough and complex understanding of culture and history. This information is readily accessible to us, but not to our students, and we rarely explain how to do contextual research. The same is true for critical articles: in the classroom, we use what we've learned from scholarly research without teaching students how to select, read, and engage with critical sources. As Kathleen McCormick says, students "lack access to the cultural, historical, literary, or theoretical discourses that would enable them actively to construct meaning from the text." Students often assume "that they themselves are incapable of reading, understanding, and certainly analyzing texts, which appear to contain secret and specialized knowledge" (59). It's not surprising, then, that students struggle to recognize the interactions among their own ideas, the ideas represented in the texts they are studying, and the information they find in contextual or critical research. If students don't understand the value of or strategies for doing research, it's no wonder they wait until late in the semester to begin their research.

Other than research, students may believe that the only step they must take before writing a paper is to read the text. They expect a thesis to appear almost magically, and once it does, they have just to find some evidence in the text, locate a few relevant quotes from critical articles, write a draft, fix typing errors, prepare a bibliography, and turn it in. They don't understand how examining a text multiple times, looking at details, reflecting on its context, or comparing it with other texts might help them gain new insights, nor have they learned the value or habit of deferring closure and letting an interpretation develop through multiple iterations. Students also don't value outlining or revision. Many expect to be able to just sit down and write. As one of the students I interviewed explained, she mulls over the text she's writing about and figures out what she wants to say about it, then locates some sources that agree with her interpretation, writes one draft, and turns it in. She's earned A's on most of the papers written with this method, so she has learned that it works.

If students' prior learning about research, writing, and the analysis of literature encourages them to approach papers in this way, some of the ways we present and structure the research paper assignment exacerbate the problem. Perhaps the most common error we make is giving assignments that provide extensive detail about technical requirements but offer minimal description of the intellectual task of doing literary research. With few exceptions, the research paper assignments I found online specified the length of the paper and how many sources students should use, and some offered reminders about format. Most described the task of the paper vaguely: "You will analyze one of the texts we've read," or "You will write a critical paper using outside sources."[2] Of course, assignment sheets are not the only information we provide. We talk in class about what we're looking for, offer advice about how to approach the task, and suggest possible topics. But often, any additional information we provide focuses on our expectations for what the final paper will look like, not on strategies for developing the analysis itself. With so little guidance, and with instructions that focus almost entirely on technicalities, it's no wonder our students don't understand that a research paper should be a reflection of inquiry, investigation, and critical thinking, nor that they don't know how to do these things.

Many literature faculty ask students to submit research proposals, usually by the middle of the term. This allows us to verify that students are pursuing appropriate topics and to offer advice about issues or sources to consider. Requiring proposals before midterm forces students to begin thinking about their papers fairly early. In some cases, though, research proposals aren't due until a few weeks before the end of the semester, giving students little time to revise their approaches or complete their projects. Our own research and writing takes months, even years, to develop, and while we ask students to take on more narrowly defined projects, we forget that, for them, the task of writing a ten-page research paper may well be comparable in difficulty to our writing a thirty-page article. Librarian Barbara Fister compares the task our students face with what we might contend with if we had to write a conference paper for an entirely different academic field:

> How would you know what kinds of research questions would be appropriate? What evidence would be considered authoritative and persuasive? What discourse conventions would you need to observe? How would you avoid totally humiliating yourself? Yet, in a sense, that's what undergraduates are faced with when asked to choose a topic and write a paper on it. They simply don't know enough to do a good job without careful preparation. It's no wonder, unfamiliar as they are with the production of scholarly knowledge, with very little sense of how texts and ideas come into being, that they often believe research is merely transcription. . . . Too often, traditional research paper assignments defeat their own purpose by implying that research is not discovery, but rather a report on what someone else has already discovered. (2)

Framing a topic, collecting and reviewing sources, developing an argument, and writing a persuasive paper are challenging tasks that students are unlikely to complete successfully in just a few weeks. Of course, students don't just need more time to work on term papers. They also need guidance that is more substantive than a long list of reminders about how to avoid plagiarism or grading criteria that ask for a "well-developed and effectively supported argument."

Requiring a proposal is a useful step in the right direction, but the wrong kind of proposal can itself contribute to students' misunderstanding of the nature of literary analysis. While some instructors ask students simply to describe their projects, many ask students to include a thesis in the proposal. This implies that literary scholarship begins with determining a thesis, and developing a paper is simply a matter of laying out the arguments and locating some supportive evidence. This contradicts several of the core elements of our strategic knowledge, especially the disposition to value complexity and ambiguity, the habit of recursive reading, and the practice of developing, exploring, and revising provisional hypotheses. For us, research is a process of exploration and discovery, not merely a matter of collecting supportive quotes. When we ask students to submit research proposals with a thesis, we encourage them to settle on a conclusion early in the process, to approach research mechanically, and to write in wooden and formulaic ways. Of course, that isn't what we intend.

I am not suggesting that we should not assign research papers. Indeed, because research-based analysis is the dominant form of literary work, and because writing in-depth papers allows students to practice moving from observation to exploration to interpretation and analysis, the research paper can play an important role in students' apprenticeship in literary thinking. The problem lies not with the task but with the way we approach it. Instead of assuming that students already know how to do effective literary research and thinking, we should take responsibility for teaching them how to do it. We cannot assume that students learn it from Introduction to Literary Studies courses, or even as part of the first-year writing sequence, nor can we count on students to figure it out on their own, with a little guidance from us in the form of comments on finished papers. If research-based analysis is the outcome of literary thinking, and if we want to put literary thinking at the heart of the English major, then attention to the process of literary inquiry should be part of all of our courses. This is important not only for those who are going on to graduate study. Developing literary habits of mind will prepare all of our students to make good observations, analyze issues and sources, and think critically about problems of all kinds.

Structuring Literary Inquiry

If we want students to write better research papers, we must help them develop the strategic knowledge necessary to develop a thoughtful, coherent, critical analysis of a literary text or topic. Four elements of strategic knowledge are both central to literary inquiry and consistently challenging for students: the ability to pose and pursue appropriate literary questions, the habit of framing and testing provisional interpretations while also exploring multiple perspectives, knowing how to learn from scholarly and primary sources, and the ability to weave together complex and coherent analyses. These elements of strategic knowledge distinguish insightful literary analysis from the formulaic imitation of literary criticism that our students too often produce. They can also help students understand the excitement (as well as the real labor) of literary research and analysis. Equally important, as students develop this kind of knowledge, they become better able to use the research paper assignment to deepen their understanding of literary texts and concepts, they become better critical thinkers and writers, and they can more effectively demonstrate their learning.

As with any other aspect of literary knowledge, we can model these ways of thinking. In class discussions and lectures, we can encourage students to consider complex and even contradictory interpretations. In reviewing students' research proposals, we can help them pose appropriate questions. We can explain what we mean when we say "use sources well." But at the core of cognitive apprenticeship is the argument that in order to learn how to engage in this kind of literary thinking, students need practice doing it, and they need feedback about how well they are doing it. We can provide that kind of learning experience by redefining the research paper assignment as an inquiry process, by scaffolding the process so that students develop their arguments more slowly and intentionally, and by offering advice as they proceed.

Drawing on the model of cognitive apprenticeship and my analysis of the problems students encounter in writing research papers, I have developed a heavily scaffolded, incremental approach that I now use in most of my advanced literature courses, including many of my graduate courses. In the "inquiry project," students spend most of the semester studying one text, author, or issue. During the term, they write four to seven short papers that look at the text from different angles. The project guides students from initial reading and observations, to posing questions, and then through several ways of reading literary texts and sources. Along with scaffolding the literary scholarship process, the inquiry project also provides multiple opportunities for me to respond individually and coach each student according to his or her needs. Usually, the project culminates in a traditional research paper, but I have sometimes asked students to finish with more informal, reflective writing. Both work well to foster an exploratory, complex analysis and a deep understanding of the text the student examines.

The inquiry project is designed to change students' approach to literary research in two specific ways. First, it slows students' interaction with their chosen texts and requires them to continue thinking about one text, in different ways, over a long period. This ensures recursive reading and thinking, and it helps students develop deeper, more complex readings. Second, guiding students through some specific different ways of thinking about a text emphasizes the process rather than the product. This process orientation is typical in first-year writing courses, but we rarely use it in upper-division literature classes. Yet English majors benefit from the incremental, scaffolded approach, from significant feedback, and from opportunities to revise. By emphasizing the process of literary inquiry, this series of assignments fosters students' literary thinking abilities and builds confidence. Students often come to feel a kind of ownership of the texts they study and the ideas they generate.

For the inquiry project, each student chooses a text, author, or issue, often from a list that I provide. Their first assignment is to keep a journal as they read the text, which is most often a novel. I ask students to observe themselves as readers, noting their own questions or responses. I also ask them to write a couple of paragraphs at the end of each reading session, reflecting on what they noticed and how they responded. Students use the observations and responses from their journals as they begin to frame questions, discuss specific issues, and develop and support their interpretations using details from the novel. The journal scaffolds important elements in literary analysis: self-reflective reading, noting details, observing anomalies and patterns. It also helps them remember how the novel changes as the reader moves from beginning to middle to end, which draws their attention to structure and effect.

In subsequent assignments, students might write about themes or patterns, or they might analyze the structure or style of a text. I tailor the short assignments to parallel the approaches we're using in discussing shared readings, and they then apply these to their own texts. For example, in a course on immigrant novels, I asked students to identify tensions in their novels, much as we were examining the themes of conflict between immigrants and native-born Americans and between generations in class discussions of Puzo's *The Fortunate Pilgrim*. What we read and how we analyze texts in class serve as a rehearsal for these assignments. In my American novels class, for example, I began with several weeks on textual analysis, because I wanted students to perform the same type of analysis on the novels they were studying. When they began work on a paper summarizing the ideas of critics, we did the same with critical articles on Faulkner's *As I Lay Dying*. The short papers provide opportunities for students to practice ways of thinking about literature while also developing deeper and more complex insights for their own inquiries. At the same time, students apply and develop what they're learning in class about themes, patterns, and critical issues by exploring how these elements work in a different text from the same period or genre.

A key task in literary inquiry is framing questions. As with every other part of the inquiry project, I prepare students for this assignment by explaining different types of literary questions and by guiding them through framing and evaluating questions in class. In the immigrant novels course, for example, students posted questions in the online discussion board about one of the novels we were reading together. In class, we reviewed a collated list of their questions, discussing which would be most generative and how we might pursue them. This preparation gave students a foundation for the questioning assignment, which asked them to pose a question, explain why it seemed significant and useful, and suggest how they might go about exploring it. In some ways, this task resembles the typical research proposal assignment, except that students don't frame questions until they have recorded their observations and responses, considered other ways of reading the text, and developed a way of thinking about questions that helps them pose their own questions more purposefully and critically.

Once students have framed questions, they are ready to begin research, but as with every other part of the process, they need guidance in order to do this well. While some students need help using research databases, most need to learn how to think about research as a reflective and exploratory process of learning about their topics. I ask them to review their inquiry questions in order to identify what kinds of information would help them develop good answers. To prepare students for this, we strategize as a class about what types of information could help us analyze the texts we're reading together. They then develop a similar "wish list" for their own projects. I tell them to imagine that they have been assigned a personal research assistant, who will collect sources for them but needs to be told what to look for. This, together with a review of the types of sources that are available (see Table 3, p. 63–64), helps them approach the research process with focus and intention.

I also want students to learn to view critical and primary sources as tools for learning, so once they've collected some sources, I ask them to begin thinking about what the sources have to offer. They write two short papers about their sources. In a critical overview, they describe the critical discussion of their text. As I explain to students, literary scholarship is essentially an ongoing but disjointed conversation among colleagues, and you can't join the conversation in a useful way unless you understand the underlying issues and positions. I assure students that I don't expect them to read everything, and I often limit the number of sources they can write about, but I ask them to describe the key themes, issues, and disagreements among the critical sources they read. Unlike an annotated bibliography, which I also sometimes assign, the critical overview paper asks students to think about how their sources fit together, rather than to view each one as an independent and isolated piece. This encourages students to view criticism as part of an ongoing debate about literary texts, and it requires them to think about the big ideas of each source rather than just zooming in on a quote or two. I also ask them to write a source comparison, in which they look more closely at two sources that offer contrasting views. In this short paper, they summarize the arguments of two critical articles, identify their points of disagreement as well as the reasons that the critics see things differently, and consider how they might use ideas from each piece. Both of these assignments help students develop their ability to read critical articles and think more carefully about how critical perspectives can help them develop and clarify their own views. They also help students understand that, by writing about literature, they can join the conversation, not just listen to it. As I tell them, doing this kind of work is like finally getting to sit at the adults table for Thanksgiving dinner.

When students write a formal paper at the end of this process, they are often surprised to discover how much of the work has already been done. They draw upon ideas from their short essays and often literally cut and paste whole sections into their rough drafts. The quality of the papers that emerge is quite good, and students are usually pleased with the final result, as am I. Several have commented that while they wrote more and worked harder for this course than for most others, they also found the final research paper easier to write.

While the inquiry project yields strong final papers, it works well even when the final product is more informal. In the immigrant novels course, students wrote informal synthesis pieces at the end, instead of a formal paper. I called these pieces "Revisiting the Inquiry," and I asked students to comment about how their initial responses and questions changed as they moved through the process and to discuss how their individual novel connected with and differed from the books we'd read together, how what they'd learned in class about the immigrant novel as a genre had (or had not) helped them notice significant issues in their novel, what conclusions they had reached, and what other directions they might want to pursue with this novel, if they had the time. Defining the project as an exploration rather than as a formal paper allowed students the freedom to pursue whatever they found in their inquiries and to accept the open-endedness and complexity of literary inquiry. In their final reflections, students acknowledged and analyzed dead ends and unexplored possibilities, and the less formal assignment invited students to write in their natural voices, rather than in self-conscious academic prose.[3] While leaving out the final critical task of translating observations, questions, and research into a critical argument, these reflective pieces were full of extended and thoughtful inquiry.

In both variations, with and without a formal final paper, the inquiry project represents students' thinking over time, demonstrating how their questions about, strategies for reading, and understanding of their chosen novel changed and deepened. Of course, English majors need to learn how to present literary arguments and follow the conventions of the discipline. But they may not need to do that in every course, and the opportunity to experience literary research in a more process-oriented, open-ended form strengthens both their abilities and their confidence.

The short assignments that make up the inquiry project provide direction and make a complex process manageable, but they don't make it easy or comfortable. Students have to try new strategies, and that always presents a risk of failure, so I'm never surprised when they express self-doubt. I try to address students' uncertainty by giving them opportunities to rehearse the new critical strategies they're learning in class before tackling them individually. But ultimately, this approach requires students to try new strategies and write papers that are quite different from what they're used to. Despite their uncertainties, students almost always respond favorably to the step-by-step design. One described the project as a "constant researching process," in which she was repeatedly "applying what I found." Because of this, she explained, "The ideas and sources I started with were almost irrelevant to my final ideas and their sources." Another wrote, "I liked doing the portfolio because I got to work at my own pace and take my time to find the answers. I liked how I was able to discover *my* answers instead of the answers that I thought [the professor] wanted me to find. . . . I was able to learn more because of this strategy because I had no fear throughout the entire process." Monica pointed out that the structure helped her to avoid becoming overwhelmed. Having small pieces due regularly, instead of just one large final project, made it impossible for her to procrastinate, she reported, but it also made the large task of researching a novel on her own feel manageable. "By just looking at the next step in front of me," she wrote, "I was successful." Mark noted that spreading out the project over the whole semester also helped him pace himself. As these comments suggest, what began for many students with uncertainty led, ultimately, to a sense of satisfaction and accomplishment.

The inquiry project gives students practice in using expert literary thinking strategies, and even though their expertise is still developing, they nonetheless experience the same shifting and deepening of their thinking that scholars go through. As they develop their own complex analyses, they also develop a stronger and more diverse literary thinking repertoire. Rikki's work on John Okada's *No-No Boy* illustrates especially well how working slowly and trying different approaches strengthened her ability to analyze the novel. She began with a traditional literary question that seemed to focus almost entirely on the text itself. "Is there some connection between style and subject matter," she asked, "or is this just the way Okada writes?" The question emerged from her experience as a reader, and she noted it first in her reading journal. As she wrote in the tensions assignment, "I liked the way it was written, but there were some parts that were confusing the first time I read them, and I had to go back to make sure I was reading it right." As she began researching, Rikki found few articles that discussed Okada's style, but she kept finding materials that examined the book as a reflection of the experiences of Japanese Americans during World War II. Initially, she saw these materials as "background information" that could help her "understand the situations of the book from the characters' points of view." As she looked more closely at the critical articles for her sources overview, Rikki identified aspects of Japanese American culture that intrigued her, and these kept leading her further away from her initial question. When she wrote her "Revisiting the Inquiry" piece, she began by reflecting that she hadn't found anything to help her with her initial question, but then she made a crucial critical move: she used the material she *had* found to look again at the issue of style. As she explained:

> The way the book is written seems to emphasize the underlying themes of disconnection and a separated self. Okada separates himself from Ichiro by not using first person, but still allows Ichiro's voice to be heard through various internal conversations he has. . . . The scattered style could be an extension of the split

feelings experienced by Ichiro, and many other Japanese living in America at the time.

If she had moved quickly from identifying a topic to writing the paper, without responding to assignments that pushed her to think in different ways, Rikki might well have either written an analysis based on her own initial reading or switched her topic entirely. But the structure of this project and the nature of the revisiting assignment encouraged her to deepen her analysis by linking it with what she had learned about the cultural context.

As Rikki's case suggests, the inquiry project can give students an experience that is more like "real" literary inquiry—an experience that begins in observation, is rooted in inquiry, relies on recursive reading and thinking, and allows the critic time to identify possible interpretations while still exploring different ways of reading a text. This incremental and open-ended approach disrupts students' usual habits and generates better, more complex critical thinking. This kind of project fosters a sense of curiosity and, especially when the project ends with critical reflections rather than a formal paper, provides students the freedom to explore without worrying that their inquiries will lead to dead ends. It encourages a sense of intellectual play, inviting students to see both novels and the resources related to them as deep and complex sources that do not always offer clear and definitive answers.[4]

Interactive Teaching

One final element makes the inquiry project work: significant individual coaching from the instructor. This kind of interactive teaching emphasizes both what we ask students to do and the response and guidance we provide to help them do better. Articles about student-centered teaching often call for teachers to stop being the sage on the stage and instead become the guide on the side. Most often, this line is used to support active, student-centered pedagogy, but students also benefit from having a personal "guide on the side," someone who provides substantive, frequent feedback. As Bourdieu writes, students can best learn how to think well by practicing "at the side of a sort of guide or trainer, who assures and reassures, who sets an example and makes corrections by specifying, in a particular situation, precepts directly applicable to a particular case" (qtd. in Brubaker 231). Bourdieu's description emphasizes interaction, and it calls to mind the artisanal model of apprenticeship, with the teacher literally sitting or standing beside students as they work. Of course, the nature of literary work makes this impossible; our students do relatively little thinking and writing while in our classrooms or offices. Even if they did, thinking is something we can see only when it is externalized—when students speak or write about their ideas. Happily, the teaching of literature offers many opportunities to respond to what students say and write in ways that can help them improve.

We do this in class all the time, albeit often quite indirectly. It's considered bad manners and poor pedagogy ever to tell a student that his idea is wrong or her question is off base. But even without such direct critique, we provide plenty of hints about which ideas and questions we see as most productive. As the students in one of my literature courses told me recently, they can tell when I agree with them by the way I respond. Sometimes, I will slightly rephrase a student's question, or I'll try to get the class to refocus or clarify an idea. These are, I think, perfectly good teaching habits. But when I describe good teaching as coaching, I mean more direct forms of advice and evaluation that help students understand how they can adjust their practice to improve their thinking. This kind of direct coaching might take many forms. As Allan Collins, John Seely Brown, and Ann Holum define it, *coaching* "consists of observing students while they carry out a task and offering hints, scaffolding, feedback, modeling, reminders, and new tasks aimed at bringing their performance closer to expert performance" (14). That does occur when we lead class discussions, but I also want to advocate for individual coaching that allows us to focus on students' specific strengths and challenges.

While we provide individual comments when we grade papers, those comments often focus on evaluation rather than on helping students develop their ideas. We can build opportunities for coaching into a course by borrowing approaches from our composition colleagues, such as requiring students to submit drafts or doing peer reviews. The more often we respond to students' individual work in progress, the more we can help them improve both their skills as literary thinkers and the quality of their final papers. This has an added advantage: students are more likely to read comments on work in progress, because they know they can use our advice, and they appreciate the attention we give them. Reading students' work as it develops also offers insight into their difficulties, so we can address them, individually or in class.

The inquiry project provides many opportunities for coaching. I respond in writing to most of the short pieces that students write as they develop their projects. This sounds like a lot of work, but because the assignments are short and I often don't assign grades, it's quite manageable. The papers range from one page to six pages, and most run only two or three pages, so they don't take long to read. Writing comments without grades is also easier for me. When I'm grading papers, I often labor over my notes to be sure that I have explained the grade clearly. In grading, I feel that I should comment on several major aspects of a paper, identifying strengths and weaknesses, discussing how the essay does or does not meet the grading criteria, and so on. When I'm responding to work in progress, I write less, I write more casually, and I focus more narrowly. I often have students submit their assignments electronically, and I add brief comments or questions using the comment feature of Word or using a different font or color. Because the style is informal and because the comments focus on how students might develop their analyses rather than on how well they have done the assignment, responding doesn't feel onerous. I feel as if I am having an extended one-on-one conversation with each student. In many cases, students write back, adding their responses to the electronic version of the paper, or they come to talk about their work. Some students argue with me. Some ask for advice on how to pursue a question I raised. Some simply express appreciation when my comments have pointed them in a productive direction. Best of all, I can often see evidence in their work that my comments have pushed them to articulate their ideas more fully and to think more critically. I almost never see that effect from traditional grading.

Not only do I enjoy the coaching process more than I do grading, working closely with students as they move through the research and writing process also makes grading the final papers easier and more enjoyable. I know the students' work well by the end of the term, so I can read the final papers quickly and assign grades with little angst or frustration. The inquiry project yields better papers, so they are more fun to read than the papers I used to receive. I also get the pleasure of reviewing students' progress and seeing how their thinking has developed. And because students have been receiving regular feedback, they have a good sense of how strong their work is. Students almost never question their grades on the inquiry project.

No doubt, teaching in this way takes more time, and I have been fortunate never to have taught more than two sections of advanced literature courses in one term, so I have time to give individual attention. Still, I have developed some strategies for providing extensive coaching in less labor-intensive ways. One is to use peer coaching. In the immigrant novels course, for example, I assigned each student to a "working group" with four or five colleagues who were studying different novels. The groups met regularly from the beginning of the semester to compare notes. At first, students complained about the makeup of the groups; a few said that they would have preferred to work with students who were studying the same book. However, because they were studying different texts, students had to describe their novels and articulate their ideas more fully than they might have if they were all analyzing the same text. Teaching others about their books helped them develop their ideas. As students began to write the more analytical papers, they shared them with their working groups and provided feedback to each other. This helped develop their metacognitive and critical abilities. Students often express doubt that their peers are capable of offering reliable feedback: "I'd rather hear what you have to say," they tell me. To help them get past this, I asked them to submit their advice to each other in writing, and I reviewed their comments quickly. Often, I was able to simply write, "I agree." Students were reassured to hear this, and when I supported their insights on each other's work, they gained confidence in themselves as critics. This was especially useful for those students who plan to become teachers of English.

The bottom line is that effective coaching takes time and energy. Yet I don't think I spend significantly more time on teaching than any of my colleagues. I never give exams, nor do I have to grade daily quizzes or in-class writing. I often use online discussions, which I read frequently, comment on occasionally, and grade holistically at midterm and the semester's end. Most of the time and energy that I give to students takes the form of individual responses to their work in progress. Interactive teaching and cognitive apprenticeship shift my attention and sometimes require more from me, but the results are so much better that the trade-off seems worthwhile. I enjoy interacting with students and their ideas, so I find teaching more fun and more rewarding when I use these approaches. Better yet, I am convinced that the time I invest in careful planning and thoughtful coaching yields significant learning of both content and strategic knowledge.

Creative Critical Design

In his book *The Crafty Reader*, Robert Scholes suggests that improving the teaching of literature requires what seems to be a fairly simple shift in focus:

> If we want our students to share with us the pleasures of the texts we admire, if we want them to enjoy the textual power that comes with mastery of our language and our culture, we need only to take seriously our responsibility as teachers of reading, which we can do by simplifying and clarifying the ways of reading we have already learned to use in our studies of English literature and culture. (2001 215)

This is a more complex task than Scholes acknowledges, but at heart, this is what the inquiry project aims to achieve. By clearly identifying a number of elements of "textual power," it "simplifies and clarifies" expert reading and interpretation. But identifying those elements is not sufficient in itself. We cannot assume that students will know how to complete each of the tasks that make up the inquiry project. We have to demonstrate and explain these strategies and give students opportunities to practice them. That will prepare them to work independently in productive ways, and that brings us back to the course planning process.

Weaving all of these strands together into a coherent and manageable course design is challenging but creative work, and like any creative effort, the process can be messy, experimental, and intuitive even as it is analytical and intentional. Planning around what to read can gener-

"messy process"

ate a fairly neat, linear course outline, and that neatness has its charms. Basing course content and schedules on learning goals, opportunities for practice, and coaching feels more like building a three-dimensional model. In this section, I want to make my own thinking a bit more visible by explaining the tools I use in designing courses. I employ a flexible, evolving planning matrix that helps me see the course from multiple angles at once. It allows me to create course structures that connect what I want students to learn with the readings, activities, and assignments that will facilitate their learning. The planning matrix captures the big picture of the semester in a complex but structured way.

I begin with a table with five columns reflecting the elements I've been discussing: content knowledge, strategic knowledge, readings, in-class activities, and assignments. Table 4 shows part of the planning matrix for my course on American novels, but it doesn't represent the process fully. I first fill in the boxes for content and strategic knowledge, putting each learning goal on its own row. Those then guide my thinking as I figure out what we should read, how we should use class time, and what assignments students will do. None of this is simple, of course. I tinker and play, refining and clarifying, moving back and forth across columns. I often move these pieces around, testing how well a strategic knowledge goal fits with different content goals or considering whether a particular reading will provide the best opportunity to explore the course content. In quite literal ways, the matrix encourages me to think about what learning experts call *alignment*. It forces me to consider whether my teaching strategies—readings, activities, and assignments—really fit my learning goals. It also ensures that I will begin course planning conceptually, with a focus on ideas rather than on tasks or texts. Finally, the matrix has the advantage of making visible all of the major elements of the course and their relationships.

What's missing from this planning matrix is any sense of time. I obviously can't plan a course without thinking about sequencing and how much time to devote to each goal, but I prefer to address these concerns only after I've considered everything else. This means that I often initially envision a course that would take two or three semesters to teach properly. Once I add a column labeled "date," I have to edit and revise. I make choices based on the learning goals, which help me determine the most important elements and what can be cut. At

Table 4. Course Planning Matrix

Content Knowledge	Strategic Knowledge	Readings	In-Class Activities	Assignments
The "great American novel" is an old and contested vision of a novel that represents American culture fully and accurately.	Analyzing the "big ideas" and literary elements of a novel—plot, character, style, structure, meaning	DeForest essay on "The Great American Novel" (1868) Two novels from that era that relate in quite different ways to "the American character": *Huck Finn* and *Portrait of a Lady*	Generating a checklist based on DeForest and a survey of how the phrase "great American novel" has been used; using that checklist to guide discussion of the novels Discussion of how the literary elements connect with the big ideas of the novels Mapping the structure of the novels Discussion of specific passages selected by students	Short essay: How is the novel you're studying "American"? How does it (or how does it not) fit into the category of a "great American novel"? Short essay: How do the literary elements of this novel contribute to (or perhaps work against) its meaning?

Table 4. Course Planning Matrix (continued)

Content Knowledge	Strategic Knowledge	Readings	In-Class Activities	Assignments
While critics debate whether any novel has ever lived up to this ideal, American novels do reflect and therefore provide insight into American culture.	Identifying historical and cultural themes through work with primary and secondary sources Connecting themes from a novel with themes from its era can help us understand both the context and the text more deeply	*Song of the Lark*	History case study: Students use selected primary and secondary materials to identify historical and cultural themes relevant to the novel In small groups, pair specific scenes or plot lines with specific contextual themes and discuss how that scene or plot element adds to students' understanding of those themes and vice versa	Short essay: How does your novel reflect or provide insight into its historical context?

this point in the planning process, I'm usually thinking about two key issues. First, how much time should I devote to each part of the course? This often requires juggling and revision. I may drop entire rows of learning goals, delete or add in-class activities, and move assignments around, based on time considerations. Second, what information from my planning process do I want to share with students? Sometimes, I choose to present the learning goals as questions rather than as concepts and statements, an approach that Wiggins and McTighe recommend. Sometimes, I define the units of the course in terms of themes. The course schedule section of my syllabus is usually a revised version of the planning matrix. Table 5 shows the schedule for the American novels course, as it appeared in the course syllabus.

I'm a course design geek. I enjoy thinking about the relationships among the elements of my courses, and I view course planning as a creative and somewhat idealistic intellectual activity. When a current course hits a snag, as almost every course (even the most carefully planned) does sometime after midterm, I start thinking about the next term's classes. But that's not just a matter of compensating for whatever my current difficulties may be. Instead, it's a way of expressing my continuing curiosity about how I can best facilitate students' learning.

The problem that Knapp posed about *how* we can bridge the gap between our expertise and our students' developing knowledge cannot be solved by making better decisions about the order in which we read texts or coming up with ever more creative assignments. It requires more deliberate and systemic thinking. It requires that we view teaching and learning as multidimensional, complex processes that benefit from intentionality and creativity, rather than as magical processes that work effortlessly for some teachers and some students. My own experience suggests another dimension to the challenge of bridging the gap: in order for faculty to make wise decisions about how to design and guide their courses, we need to understand our students—their prior experiences, their assumptions, their difficulties, and their habits. All of the ideas I've laid out so far are based not only on reading and conversations about learning but also on my own investigations into how my students think. The more I understand about them and their work, the more effectively I can plan and implement good teaching.

Table 5. Course Schedule

Date	Reading	Content Knowledge	Strategic Knowledge	Papers and Projects Due
1/15	John William DeForest, "The Great American Novel" Jay Parini, "Introduction," *Promised Land*	What makes a novel significant?		
1/20–1/29	*Huckleberry Finn*	What's American about this novel? How does this novel represent/reflect American culture?	reading for plot and character	
2/3–2/12	*Portrait of a Lady*	What are the limits of "Americanness"? How is James an "American" novelist?	reading beyond plot and character —style and structure	2/3: reading journal
2/17–2/26	*The Song of the Lark*	The novel as historical lens: what can we learn by reading this novel as a historical text?	contextual analysis	2/26: analysis of elements— plot, character, style, and structure
3/3–3/19	*The Bluest Eye*	novels as social commentary	contextual analysis	3/19: mid-term discussion, board evaluations

Table 5. Course Schedule (continued)

Date	Reading	Content Knowledge	Strategic Knowledge	Papers and Projects Due
3/24– 4/2	*Uncle Tom's Cabin*	novels as political advocacy	contextual analysis	4/2: *UTC* research presentations
4/7– 4/16	*As I Lay Dying*	innovations in the form— style and structure	reading beyond plot and style	4/9: your novel in context
4/21– 4/28	*On the Road*	innovations in the form— content and structure	connecting plot and style with context	4/28: the critical conversation about your novel
4/30– 5/7	Presentations			5/7: complete portfolio

4 ■ Analyzing Students' Learning

How do we know how well students understand the content and strategies we teach in literature courses? Even more important, when students have difficulty with ideas or skills, how can we determine what's going wrong? So much of learning is invisible. We may be able to see that students did not explain clearly the connection between a line of text and a theme in a poem, but what we really want to know is why. What were they thinking? How did their approach to the poem generate this vague connection? Or is the gap a matter of writing—perhaps they ran into difficulty in articulating the connection, not in recognizing it? The work that students produce provides a visible manifestation of their knowledge, but if literary understanding involves ways of thinking, then what we really want to know is not just what students can do but how they are thinking. We want, in other words, to get inside their heads, to read their minds.

Of course, we can't actually do that. But we can look closely at students' work through a framework that views errors and difficulties as evidence of ways of thinking rather than simply as reflections of lack of effort or ability. We can also talk with students about their thinking, both as they are working with a text and in retrospect. Scholars of teaching and learning advocate for more attentive, critical analysis of students' work as evidence of their learning, and they offer methods that can help us work with students to gain insight into their thinking. We may not be able to read students' minds, but if we take the time to pursue critical questions about their learning, we can understand their thinking more fully, and that can help us teach more effectively.

Like many of my colleagues in the scholarship of teaching and learning (SoTL), I see research on students' learning as fitting into two of the three standard categories of faculty work: scholarship and teaching. Analyzing students' understanding, investigating their difficulties, and evaluating strategies for effective teaching involve intellectual processes and strategies that are similar to what I do in literary research, though with a focus on students' texts rather than literary works. Making this part of my research agenda not only integrates two core parts of my professional life, it also contributes to the ongoing critical discussion about teaching and learning in our discipline and across higher education. What one person discovers in studying her students' learning may prove useful to others on both a practical and a theoretical basis. This work may also contribute to a cultural shift in our profession. Professors and critics have long lamented that teaching is not taken more seriously or valued more highly at many universities. Analysis of the culture of higher education may not be enough to change that. Taking teaching more seriously ourselves can. As more scholars in the disciplines publish and present their research on students' learning, we demonstrate that teaching is important intellectual work and that critical engagement with teaching can be a core part of academic life.

I also believe that this kind of analysis is worth doing regardless of whether it leads to publication. The ideas about learning that underlie this approach and the insights we gain by analyzing our students' learning are valuable even if we never share our findings with anyone else. Asking critical questions about students' learning can help us teach better, and it can make teaching more satisfying. Analyzing students' learning can help us identify and diagnose patterns of difficulty, develop effective teaching strategies, and work more effectively with our students. It is useful in preparing materials for tenure and promotion, or simply responding to colleagues' questions about why we teach in particular ways, because it provides both a rationale and evidence of the effectiveness for our ways of teaching. It can also help us assess the effectiveness of our programs.

From Anecdote to Analysis

The standard model for writing about English studies pedagogy is what we might call, to borrow a phrase from Lee Shulman, the "what-works" article. In a what-works essay, the writer describes a strat-

"what-works"

egy for teaching a particular theme or type of course. We might not describe these as research articles, however, because they tend to involve little investigation of particular texts or sources. Rather, they tend to be, as Mariolina Salvatori has suggested, anecdotal. We write stories about teaching that we hope will inspire others to try our approaches.

As Salvatori notes, these anecdotes are engaging and useful, but they often leave us without a clear understanding of student learning. She advocates turning our attention to "students' work, their cultural capital, and their learning as a litmus test for the theories that inform a teacher's approach" (298). In other words, she encourages us to go beyond describing what works to analyzing students' learning as evidence that can help us understand why it works. As Randy Bass and I wrote in 2008, in a study of articles on teaching literature from the journal *Pedagogy*, literary scholars have not yet made close reading of students' work part of our practice in thinking about teaching. Such a focus on student learning would, we suggested, be useful and productive for our discipline, because it would help us develop a shared language for and a deeper critical understanding of the nature of literary learning. Looking closely at evidence of students' learning can also help us question our own assumptions and gain fresh insights into how students think about literature. Analyzing students' learning can give us better answers to the questions we all wrestle with. Why don't students do the reading? Why don't they do better research, or use the research more effectively? How can I help them make sense of theory? These questions point to core concerns of our discipline, not only in the classroom but in our disciplinary research as well.

The scholarship of teaching and learning provides a broad framework and some guidelines to help us interpret and evaluate students' learning effectively. Many English faculty get nervous about the idea of doing classroom research, perhaps because the dominant model for educational scholarship is based in the social sciences. You may not want to do quantitative analysis or read a bunch of articles written in the academic jargon of psychology or education. Neither do I. While social science models have had a powerful influence on SoTL, I believe that the scholarly practices of literary studies translate well to the analysis of student learning. Close reading, identifying patterns, considering connections between text and context, and applying theoretical concepts to specific cases—all practices that are common in literary research—work well as tools for examining student learning. We can adapt techniques from other fields, but we can also draw on the methods we already use well.

Like any research, SoTL often begins with observation and questioning. While we sometimes analyze students' learning in order to find out how well a particular teaching technique or assignment works, for me the most useful work always begins with problems. This focus on problems may seem, well, problematic. First, it emphasizes students' errors and difficulties rather than their strengths and successes, so it can feel negative. While this approach does focus on deficits, it also operates on the assumption that a major source of students' difficulties is not their limitations but how we teach. In other words, problems are not necessarily the fault of students, and we as teachers have the insight, power, and responsibility to address them. Another potential difficulty with focusing on problems comes when we think about SoTL as research that can lead to publication or presentation, because none of us wants to put our problems on display. As Bass points out in one of the foundational articles of the SoTL movement, we see problems as essential for our disciplinary research, but having a problem in the classroom is a cause for embarrassment. Bass explains, however, that investigating classroom difficulties helped him to stop thinking of them as personal failures and begin to see teaching as "a set of problems worth pursuing as an ongoing intellectual focus" (1999). When we take teaching problems seriously, we gain fresh perspectives on both our teaching and our literary research. Faculty resist exploring problems for another reason: we are more interested in solutions. Most of us have plenty of theories about why students struggle as well as interesting ideas about what to do about it, and so we tend to move quickly from noticing a problem to developing a new assignment or strategy to address it. But if we don't understand what's going wrong, we can waste time with inappropriate solutions. Taking the time to examine problems critically can help us develop better solutions. At the same time, it can help us gain broader insight into students' learning in our discipline.

Let me offer an example. In a SoTL workshop a few years ago, I talked with Andrew Mills, a philosopher who wanted to help his students learn to pose what he called "philosopher's questions." He was frustrated with the questions his students posed: they didn't fit the material, weren't appropriate for the course, or were simply not well framed. Of course, he had an idea for how to solve the problem (a series of exercises that would give students practice posing questions), and he was anxious to collect evidence to show that his approach worked. Discussion in the workshop persuaded him that before he could design an effective solution he needed to understand more fully both the questions students were asking and what he was looking for. Over the next couple of years, he spent time looking more closely at students' questions and thinking more carefully about what he meant by "philosopher's questions." He realized that students defined *philosophical* quite differently than he did: they saw questions about people's motivations or personal histories as philosophical, while Mills was hoping for questions that addressed ways of thinking, logic, and assumptions. That helped him not only develop a better strategy, but also construct a persuasive argument for why his strategy worked, ultimately resulting in an article about why questions are important in philosophy and how to teach students how to pose good ones.

As Mills's story suggests, while it's important to think critically about the nature of the problem itself, we also need to examine evidence and sources that will help us understand it better. In literary research, this often means reading both related literary texts and critical discussions, and the same is true in SoTL. We can study the texts of learning—students' papers, interviews, classroom questionnaires, students' reflections—much as we do a literary text: analyzing the words and phrases, reading between the lines, reading against the grain. Such readings can yield interpretations of how the text itself reveals students' understanding, how the context influences the text, or how the text reflects a theory about how people learn. Other critical views, both theoretical discussions about how students learn and concrete examples, such as articles about how others teach a similar course, provide a conceptual framework to help us read our own students' work in new ways. Just as with a literary analysis, we should support interpretations of student learning with primary evidence as well as discussion of the context and integration with theoretical models.[1]

Unlike literary analysis, SoTL often culminates in new teaching strategies and assignments, and these are then tested with more research and refined over time. But even this is not entirely unfamiliar; in literary research, the insights from one project often generate fresh questions that engage us in new research. The entire process of addressing a significant problem might take several years, though small-scale investigations can use the same approach to analyze more specific problems. For example, my first questions about my students' disappointing research papers led me into research that spanned a decade, conducted in seven different courses, as I moved from exploring a problem to testing various ways of addressing it, to considering new problems and thus new strategies.

The approaches outlined here can provide insight into whatever questions or problems you encounter, on whatever scale you wish to work. It's true that even a small-scale exploration will take some time, especially when you first begin to use these ideas. While we can adapt familiar methods like close reading and reviewing relevant critical literature to SoTL, doing this work with a different type of text and in a context in which we are so deeply implicated is new, as is the very idea of shifting our focus to learning. If we incorporate less familiar tools, like questionnaires and interviews, the process may feel strange, especially at first. Yet while we may use new methods for collecting material to analyze, the critical reading and analysis skills that we use in studying literature will serve us well as we read texts that reflect student learning.

It's neither necessary nor wise to begin with a large-scale SoTL project. Improving the teaching of literature can begin quite simply when we stop focusing on how we teach and begin to ask how our students are learning and why. In other words, this is as much about mindset as it is about research methods. It means looking at students' learning not only in terms of success or failure but also in terms of process and perspective. It means seeking real, complex answers to the question "Why don't they get it?" rather than assuming that the problem is students' ability or effort. We can begin to improve our teaching by paying closer attention to our students' learning, and the approaches I lay out below offer some tools for doing that.

[handwritten margin note: how are ppl. learning? not how do I teaching.]

Research Strategies

Historian Lendol Calder titles a workshop he gives on the scholarship of teaching and learning "What Were They Thinking?" The title implies the sort of perplexed, almost sarcastic phrasing we might use when someone paints a house an especially ugly color or professes a love for a cheesy movie. That is what we really want to know when we begin to look closely at students' learning, but of course we can't see inside their heads. We have to deduce students' thoughts and thinking processes, but how? We can try to catch them in the act of thinking, though that's difficult. Alternatively, we can look at their work, the materials that result from their thinking. We can also ask them to comment on their own learning or pose questions whose answers might demonstrate their understanding. And we can turn to the wisdom of other scholars. These strategies complement each other, providing different and relevant insights that help us understand problems, develop solutions, and find out how well a solution works. Perhaps none will quite let us read students' minds, but they come as close as we're likely to get.

Thinking in the Moment

Thinking is an inherently silent, invisible process, but a number of scholars have tried to capture it, primarily through a research tool called think-alouds. In a think-aloud, a student or faculty member is given a text or problem and asked to vocalize their thoughts as they begin to work with it. This can be awkward, because we are simply not in the habit of putting our thoughts into words in this immediate way, and often what we're thinking doesn't even take the form of clear sentences and paragraphs. Further, thinking out loud can feel risky; participants—especially students—may worry that they are "thinking wrong" or that some thoughts are not relevant. In the most formal version, think-alouds are conducted almost like an interview, and researchers often record them for later analysis. Although useful for research, this format can also contribute to students' anxiety about the tool. While imperfect, research using this technique suggests that it can help us identify the thinking habits that contribute to students' difficulties. Sam Wineburg's research on the differences between how scholars and students approach a first reading of an unfamiliar historical document highlighted a significant gap, one that has proven useful not only for historians but also for scholars in other fields. Georgetown mathematics professor Jim Sandefur used think-alouds to gain insight into how his students approach mathematical problem solving, and he discovered that students encounter difficulties because they try to guess at solutions rather than analyzing the problem.[2]

Because thinking out loud is such an unusual practice, we have to train students to do it. We can demonstrate it ourselves or use it in class or in assignments, giving students opportunities to practice. Educational research suggests that such assignments actually help students learn by making them more aware of their own thinking processes. While being recorded and observed can create discomfort, with some preparation and patience, students can show us at least part of what's going on in their minds.

In my research for this book, I asked both faculty and students to read and respond to an unfamiliar poem, to tell me what they thought about as they tried to make sense of it. Despite the awkwardness, their comments revealed some key differences between how faculty and students approach poetry. For faculty, the language itself drew primary attention. Almost every faculty member repeated key phrases or words in the poem, sometimes noting that a phrase was "nice" or "interesting," suggesting that they had noticed it but hadn't yet figured out why it was significant. They also identified connections across lines and focused on core linguistic and conceptual tensions within the text. They didn't try to describe the poem's speaker or its situation until after they'd spent considerable time examining its language, images, and structure. Students, on the other hand, often began by saying that they didn't even know where to begin. Most then proceeded to explicate the poem, trying to paraphrase the lines or offering a description of the speaker's state of mind or suggesting a possible scenario, with relatively little attention to specific words or phrases. Faculty seemed comfortable not settling on an interpretation and focusing on language, while students treated the poem as a story, with language taking a subordinate position. For the students, it seemed, the point of reading the poem was to figure out what was happening. For the faculty, the point was to think about how the language, images, and structure worked together to create a mood. The think-aloud thus revealed a significant and useful difference, one that suggests the potential benefit of encouraging students to delay translating a poem into a narrative and to examine language more closely.

While think-alouds are usually conducted as individual interviews, we can adapt the concept to a variety of forms. One situation in which people are more likely to put their thoughts into words is the small-group discussion. I use these frequently in my classes, for a variety of reasons, and they can yield information much like what a formal one-on-one think-aloud provides. Such group work can be videotaped, and while that can make people self-conscious, the results are still useful. Alternatively, I sometimes ask one student in the group to take notes on how the group approaches the question or task I've given them. While both approaches have limitations, they also allow me to see what ideas, focuses, concepts, and methods students bring to analyzing texts. For example, videotapes of students working in pairs on a website, together with their notes about what they looked at, helped me explore what they thought was significant and what associations they made with the material. It also helped me understand where students began and how they proceeded in working with the site.

Video recordings of class discussions can also show us at least some of students' thinking in process, and simply capturing what really happens in class discussion and small-group work is useful. As more than one critic has pointed out, teachers are surprisingly willing to hear and recall what we choose. What felt like a lively class discussion might turn out, when I review the recording, to have involved only a few students. Equally important, the act of leading a class discussion is absorbing, so the teacher often simply doesn't notice some of what happens. A review of students' comments and questions can provide insight into what they focus on, what assumptions they make, and how their ways of talking about texts change over time.

Students can also show their thinking in writing, as Sharona Levy has demonstrated by asking students to identify difficult lines in course readings by using the comment feature of Word (in Bass and Eynon). The "difficulty paper" that Mariolina Salvatori and Pat Donohue describe in their book *The Elements (and Pleasures) of Difficulty* offers a similar glimpse into students' thinking processes. The reading journal assignment I use similarly asks students to pay attention to and record their own reading and responses, and these can be analyzed much as we read any other written text. Whether in a video or audio recording or in writing, individually or in small groups, variations on the think-aloud can capture much of what our students are thinking as they work with texts. In addition, all of these examples begin as assignments and exercises to help students learn, but they also provide resources for our analysis of students' learning.

Demonstrations of Learning

Think-alouds can be useful, but they are not the easiest method for gaining insight into students' learning. For that, we need look no further than the stacks of papers on our desks. Students demonstrate their learning, the results of their thinking, in their written work. While papers and other written materials can't tell us the whole story of the ideas and habits that shape students' work, they show us quite a lot about students' ways of thinking about literature. They are also readily available and abundant—almost too much so. In any course, students create a variety of products, each of which might reflect a different moment in or aspect of their thinking. They may write a series of short essays, participate in an online discussion, write informally in class, and, of course, write research papers. To examine all of this from even a single course could be overwhelming. The challenge, then, is to choose a useful set of materials to examine and to read them with fresh eyes.

Selecting the right examples depends, of course, on what you want to find out. If I am interested in how the exercises and practice work that we do in class contribute to students' ability to write a strong analysis, I might compare students' comments in online discussions, where they use strategic tools informally, with their final papers. Do the ways of thinking that we use in practice show up in their more formal writing? Do they apply these on their own, when I'm not prompting them to do so? If I am interested in how students' thinking about a particular theme changes over time, I might follow the online discussion or a series of informal writing assignments, looking at how the class as a whole or even a few students write about that theme. If I want to understand the difficulties students have using literary research effectively, I might analyze a set of final papers, annotated bibliographies, or research journals, or I could look at all three—the multiple moments when students engage with critical materials.

What we look at also depends on what we have. While it can be useful to know from the outset what you want to collect for later analysis, in practice I find that I rarely know at the start of a term what I'm going to want to examine later. Sometimes, I've simply had to work with whatever materials I had left at the end of the term; students often don't bother to pick up final papers, and increasingly students submit at least some of their work electronically, so these documents are easy to retrieve. I've contacted students after a course was over to request copies, and most students respond helpfully. In other words, while being deliberate and strategic is wise, a lack of advance planning shouldn't keep you from looking critically at what students' work shows about their learning. That said, I've developed the habit of collecting and responding to most student work electronically, in part because I find that I offer more helpful comments using a word processing program than when I scribble in the margins. I also often use online discussions. Both formats, which I use primarily because of the learning benefits to students, have also served my needs as a researcher, leaving me with a rich collection of students' formal and informal writing over the course of the semester.

This may sound overwhelming, and collecting data on student learning can easily fill our office shelves or our hard drives with more material than we will ever need. Keep two points in mind. First, collecting data that reflect students' learning need not involve doing anything other than teaching your course and holding on to some materials. Second, you can learn much by looking at the work of just a few students or at a few key moments in the course. In order to make either an informal exploration or a larger research project work, you must be selective. Begin with one assignment. Look at just a few students' work. From a class of twenty, I might select a half dozen papers to reread closely. Depending on what I'm interested in, I could select a set of the best papers, perhaps to identify the qualities that make them work, or I might look at a range of papers to help clarify the differences between a good response and a less effective one. I might follow three or four students across a term, looking for moments when their thinking changed or to find out how their work improved. I could focus on the online discussion posts from one week, looking for the difficulties students encountered in trying to apply a specific concept or strategy. If you haven't done this kind of analysis before, I suggest that you start small in order to make the exploration process manageable. You may also want to try analyzing different types of writing to discover which provides the most useful evidence for your own concerns. You may find that, for you, students' journals reveal more than finished papers, or you may discover that you learn most by examining multiple pieces by a single student. The only rule in selecting students' work to study is that the pieces you choose should have something to show about the problem you're exploring.

Having gathered a reasonable set of texts to study, I sit down to read. Or, I should say, to reread. Reading for grading requires a different kind of thinking than reading to analyze students' learning, and I always recognize patterns more clearly when I have a little distance from the course and can take my time. I often read through a whole set of materials once, just to refresh my memory and get an overview. From there, I look more closely at specific examples, marking significant passages in each text and taking notes. As I work through the marking and note-taking process, I begin to identify patterns and analyze what I'm seeing. Because I find this to be the most useful method in my SoTL toolkit, I want to take some time to show you how it works, using two examples from my American novels course.

The course used the inquiry project model outlined in chapter 3, beginning with a reading journal. For the first essay, students analyzed the style, structure, plot, and character of a contemporary American novel. When I planned the course, I assumed that most of my students would have some prior experience with and knowledge about studying novels. Specifically, I expected that they would be comfortable talking about characters, plot, and, to a lesser extent, style. I planned to spend the first third of the course working with these elements and introducing the related concept of structure, but I thought of all of this as reinforcing existing knowledge, not as presenting new knowledge. In class, we defined each of these concepts, and we used them to analyze how, for example, Mark Twain's and Henry James's writing styles each shaped the reading experience and reflected the ideas and themes of their novels, and how the temporal and geographical structures of *Huck Finn* and Willa Cather's *Song of the Lark* intertwined physical travel with individual development, but in different ways. Students practiced using these concepts both in class and in online discussions. Yet they expressed uncertainty about how to write the paper, and I was disappointed by the quality of the papers overall.

I wanted to understand what had gone wrong, and in order to do that, I looked at two sources: the reading journals in which students took informal notes about their observations and responses as they read the novels they were studying, and a set of typical papers. The journals would give me some insight into students' thinking processes: what they noticed and what they thought about the scenes, phrases, and references that seemed important to them. The finished analyses would show me how students used the four concepts and would help me identify the kinds of difficulties they encountered in applying them.

The reading journal is one of my favorite assignments, and students often tell me that it is both the most unusual and most useful part of the course. It's a fairly simple but unfamiliar and sometimes awkward task for students to take notes as they read a novel. They write down questions and responses that occur as they read, and they write a journal entry reflecting on their own ideas and attitudes after each reading session. As they work on later papers, students almost always find these notes useful, because they help them find their way back to significant passages, to remember how aspects of the book affected them initially, and, in many cases, to identify questions and issues to explore. As one student wrote in an anonymous survey, "It was much easier to write longer analysis papers when I had the reading journal with my observations in front of me." The journals also give me a sense of how students think about novels early in the course.

I reviewed seven reading journals, chosen because they reflected somewhat different ways of approaching the task. I coded the journals using a notation technique that I've adapted from social science methodology. In the social sciences, *coding* involves identifying terms or other patterns that you want to track, marking these when they appear in the text, and then analyzing—often quantitatively—how and how frequently each is used. Many anthropologists and sociologists use complex software packages to code transcripts of their ethnographic interviews, for example, and the process for them is highly systematic and time-consuming. What I do is much more informal, more like a shorthand way of taking notes. Instead of making notes in the margins, I use different colored pens or highlighters to mark sections of the journals to indicate where students focused on plot and character, style, the structure of the novel, or their own feelings, attitudes, or connections. My color-coded marks show quickly and graphically the content of students' observations, responses, and questions.

The most common focus in the journals is on plot and character. In some cases, students note which events or aspects of the characters seem significant, while others frame questions about the plot, the significance of a scene, or why characters behave in certain ways. Most of the journals note at least a few elements of style—words or phrases that stood out, allusions, symbols, or tone. Students often express their feelings about the text—not only whether they like a book or find it boring, but also their empathy for or frustration toward characters and even the way the book connects with their own experiences. In a few cases, students note structural elements: patterns such as how each chapter begins, how meaning is developed as the novel progresses, or the relationship between different sections of a book.

The complexity and perspective in students' comments on plot and character differed widely. Elise made very brief notes about Annie Proulx's *The Shipping News:*

- Confusion of Petal and Quoyle's marriage
- He is taken advantage of at the paper
- Partridge is very smart but limited . . . stuck in his job as copy editor.

These bullet points say little about what she was thinking or why these points seemed significant to her, though in the long run, even her quite terse notes proved useful. For Sheri, writing about Chuck Palahniuk's

Fight Club, the novel raised many questions about plot: "What exactly happened in the narrator's apartment?" "Is the mechanic in charge now?" In contrast, Katie noted events or aspects of characters, but she also regularly speculated about them, questioned their significance, or noted her own responses:

> My first impression of the two aunts—they have no idea how to handle kids if they count hours until bed and they sure can talk. They keep switching between topics without having very much to say.
> The aunts have really great characterization showing how they don't fit in. I like the line about growing out of shoes messing with the lifestyle. They probably won't last much longer in this story.

As the second paragraph of Katie's notes about Marilynne Robinson's *Housekeeping* shows, she often integrated comments about style with thoughts about plot and character. For her, these elements intertwine. While that interconnection would become the central theme of Katie's study of the novel, for other students, journal notes about plot present a summary of the novel but do not record their thoughts.

In commenting on style, students often just note words or images that stand out, sometimes because they're confusing, sometimes because they're just interesting. Elise noted that Proulx uses unusual names, while Sheri noticed Palahniuk's repetition of words like "switch" and "changeover." Some students focused on allusions and repeated images that seemed to have special significance, like the knots that Elise noticed in *The Shipping News* or Krista's attention to references to Greek mythology in *Middlesex* by Jeffrey Eugenides. Only two or three students discussed how style affected their reading experience, however. Jenn recognized early on that Philip Roth's use of many names in *The Counterlife* confused her, and she later noted that his way of representing dialogue made a scene in which two characters converse hard to follow. Elise noted that the "choppy" style in Proulx sometimes created confusion, while Katie returned multiple times in her journal to notes about how Robinson's detailed, evocative descriptions shaped her own feelings:

> Everything about the flood destruction is highly imagistic. I can just smell all the rotting furniture. . . . I understand that everything's flooded and wet and there's nothing they can do about it.

I do like the writing she's using to describe the situation but she is dragging things a little.

As with students' comments on character and plot, not articulating their thoughts about the significance of a style element doesn't necessarily prove that they weren't thinking about it. On the other hand, I did see a correlation between students' habit or ability to not merely take note of something interesting but also reflect on its significance and the strength of their later analytical writing. Katie, who offered some of the most thoughtful commentaries in her reading journal, also wrote some of the stronger papers in the course, and she ultimately earned a solid A.

But different styles of response also reflected students' personalities, habits of mind, and attitudes. I saw this most clearly in Jay's journal on Bret Easton Ellis's *American Psycho,* which reflected his personality; it's full of "notes to self" and funny comments about the novel's pop culture references:

- I hate to agree with Bono on anything, but he sums it all up when he says, "A hero is an insect in this world." This rings true because we spend too much time focusing on the monsters like Bateman.

- Note to self . . . must get a copy of Bruce Willis's "The Return of Bruno." [ellipses in the original]

A few of Krista's responses to *Middlesex* also showed how she brought her own experience and perspective to her reading:

I grew up attending a Greek Orthodox Church, so it is very interesting for me to read these descriptions of one. It's amazing how similar the church being described is to the church I attended. I love being able to connect with a book like this and feel like I can relate it to pieces of my life.

In a somewhat different way, Jenn phrased many of her responses to *The Counterlife* in terms of her feelings about its events and characters. She expressed sorrow, anger, frustration, and amusement at different points, often linking her response to a specific scene.

The journals give me a glimpse into how students think about a novel as they read—what they notice, what seems significant, how they respond—but they don't tell the whole story. Despite some limitations, reviewing students' reading journals helped me realize a few things. First, students are not used to thinking about how texts work as they read. As one wrote in the anonymous survey:

> I really didn't quite realize how my brain took in the information in a novel and processes it. It wasn't until this assignment that I had ever been asked to think about what I was reading on such a macro level; even I didn't think to ask myself that. It taught me to raise more questions, think about the words more, and catch significant details that I wouldn't otherwise have seen.

It seems reasonable to assume that when engaging in this unfamiliar activity of reading attentively, students would rely on the aspects of the novel with which they felt most comfortable. For most of them, plot and character seemed most familiar and significant. Most journal comments focused on what happens in the novel, including the actions and feelings of the characters. Most students were also fairly comfortable reading responsively, in the sense that almost all commented in the journal about their own emotional and intellectual responses to the novels. While some students noticed aspects of style, few seemed to think about how style works other than to comment on issues of clarity. Almost no one seemed to see style in relation to the ideas or mood of a novel.

When I turned to students' essays, I selected three typical B papers. I didn't choose A papers, because I wasn't worried about the few students who had done very well. Most of the students whose papers had earned a C or below seemed to have misunderstood the assignment, while the mid-range students got the gist of it but faltered in the execution. I chose three essays that had typical strengths and weaknesses. In rereading, some clear patterns emerged. First, all three students used style and character as their primary concepts, though they also alluded to other elements, and all three used specific elements of style. Second, while they described style reasonably well, two of the three failed to articulate or describe the qualities of character well. Third, with both style and character, students had difficulty moving from description to analysis. They could describe what happens in the text, point to details, or offer illustrative quotes. They also made some critical moves toward explaining why these concepts and details matter, but they rarely did so effectively. Their analysis just didn't come through clearly. The details they provided suggest that they understood the basic concerns of these concepts, but their incomplete analyses suggest difficulties in application. Did the difficulty lie in their ability to interpret the text, or did it lie in their ability to communicate their thinking? I looked more closely at the three papers for clues.

Doug displayed examples of two ways that students run into difficulty in developing an analysis. In the second paragraph of his paper on Michael Chabon's *The Amazing Adventures of Kavalier and Clay*, he described Chabon's tone as "nostalgic and whimsical," but he offered no illustrative example or explanation. He did note, however, that this tone is appropriate for the book's setting, pointing to its 1930s and '40s context. He noticed an important aspect of the book but either didn't think it required illustration or couldn't think of a good example. He went on to fall into the opposite trap: offering an example without clearly explaining its significance. He introduced a two-sentence descriptive quote by saying, "Chabon's prose is beautifully crafted and spun into a perfect weave of fun yet impressive brilliance." He followed the quote by commenting that it is "just one example of Chabon's impressive imagery and execution." The almost gushing language that Doug used—"beautifully crafted," "spun into a perfect weave," "impressive imagery"—suggests that he saw the quality of Chabon's style as both good and significant. But why? What did he see in the quote that makes it "beautifully crafted"? What is so impressive about the imagery here? Doug liked Chabon's style but had difficulty either identifying, naming, or explaining the qualities that make it so appealing. On the other hand, he recognized that style includes multiple elements, and he used some of them quite well. For example, he offered a clear discussion of how Chabon uses allusion:

> Another genius vehicle for allusion is the character Sam Clay and his association with the Golem of Jewish myth. Golems, made of "clay," were protectors of the Jewish peoples and would assume

the qualities of men and play here. This allusion lives in Sam's protection of Joe, having escaped Nazi-occupied Prague to America, and helping him find solace in the art of comics. Once Joe no longer has any need for protection and comfort, Sammy loses necessity and escapes the picture, much like the Golem.

I find it telling that Doug's voice in this strong section lost some of the stylistic excess that appeared in other sections. When he had something concrete and clear to say, he moved fairly quickly away from flourishes like "genius vehicle" to more ordinary, clear, academic prose.

Like Doug, Jenn focused on style and character, though she incorporated some discussion of plot into her style analysis. She named several specific stylistic tools that Roth uses in *The Counterlife,* though she didn't explain how he uses them or why they matter. After simply listing some of them, she went on to focus on one, the way he constructs unreliable narration by revisiting the same plot elements but changing what happens. She described this style briefly, giving concrete examples from two sections of the book, and she suggested that this pattern connects with the novel's themes of deception and exploration of the self. While some more general discussion of the novel might have supported this claim more fully, the basic ideas were clear here. But when Jenn went on to discuss vocabulary and tone, the analysis was less well developed. Like Doug, she offered quotes to make her case, but she didn't discuss them. In a three-sentence paragraph, she presented but didn't fully explain what she saw: after a first sentence suggesting that the vocabulary and tone used by key characters change in different parts of the novel, she introduced and quoted two lines from the same character but from different sections of the book. But how did she see that difference? Why did she think it matters? If the two lines were obviously different, that might have been a sufficient or at least a good start, though I'd still want to see her offer some comment on how this style element works in the novel. But they are not. Because of this, the claim of the paragraph was both unclear and unpersuasive.

Jenn went on to discuss the novel's three main characters, describing each one without ever commenting on how the qualities of the characters relate to the themes or effects of the novel. She clearly recognized that the nature of these characters matters, and she used details from the text to develop her discussion of each character. She noted, for example, Roth's use of his alter ego, Nathan Zuckerman, as well as that character's stability relative to others in the novel, but she didn't even acknowledge that there might be a relationship between that stability and the themes she introduced earlier. She was clearly able to describe characters, and she supported her discussions of them by citing specific scenes or quotes. But as with some of her style discussions, she didn't explain why these elements seemed significant to her.

Elise did a good job of identifying style features in her analysis of *The Shipping News,* noting the fragmented and imagistic narrative style, Proulx's use of knots as a recurring motif, and the way the author gives characters distinctive voices. She also suggested that Proulx's style helps to develop the characters, noting that Quoyle's style reflects his job as a reporter, while the style in the sections focusing on Petal uses "vocabulary that is simple and language that is not complex," as fits a child. Indeed, Elise integrated style and character especially well. And yet, throughout her essay, she seemed to have difficulty articulating her thoughts. Her ideas surfaced almost indirectly, even when she was commenting on the details she offered. In presenting a three-sentence quote describing the scenery from early in the novel, Elise wrote, "Proulx uses direct, fragmented language," a fairly accurate description of the quality of the example: "It was spring. Sodden ground, smell of earth. The wind beat through twigs, gave off a greenish odor like struck flints." But in trying to explain why this style matters, she stumbled, offering vague explanations: the language "create[s] an original experience of the setting" so "the setting does not lose any context. The fragments allow the reader to absorb each description fully before moving on to the next." She went on to suggest that Proulx's style reminded her of Browning's. She seemed to be trying to explain how Proulx creates a scene that we can imagine clearly, that lets us feel as if we were there, and that slows down our reading with concrete language, but she had difficulty putting this into words. She noticed an important style element of the text, and I think she probably understood its significance, but she seemed not to have a vocabulary for explaining it.

Looking at the journals and essays together leads me to two insights. First, as the journals show, few of these students are in the habit of thinking about the relationship between the way a text is written and the reading experience, except when a text creates problems. Even then, they can readily identify stylistic and structural elements, as well as how a writer develops character, but they have difficulty explaining the effects or significance of those aesthetic elements. Our class discussions may have strengthened their ability to notice these aspects of a text, but these students were not yet able to interpret them effectively. Perhaps my assumption that students already knew how to use these elements was wrong? Perhaps I need to teach them to understand the reading process as involving not just noticing and responding but also explaining the relationship between the two?

Second, Elise's struggle to articulate how the elements she noticed worked makes me wonder how much of the problem lies not in how students think about the relationship between the form of a text, its effects, and its meanings, but rather in their own writing and vocabulary. Perhaps the breakdown lies not in students' understanding of the nature of style or character, or even in their ability to recognize that these elements help to shape both the readers' experience and the meaning of a novel, but rather in finding ways to articulate that relationship. I've been focusing my teaching on helping students use these concepts, but I've spent almost no time on how to construct an argument based on them, nor on how to explain clearly how they work. Perhaps I need to spend more time discussing how to write well about literature?

As this example shows, reading students' work to identify patterns of learning involves little in the way of special tactics or tools. Nor must it take significant amounts of time. Reading students' work as evidence of learning simply means looking again, in a slightly different way, at the written materials in which students show us what they do and do not understand. In this case, the hour I spent rereading the journals, the second hour I spent rereading the essays, and most important, the practice of thinking about them as representative texts (rather than as evidence of individual effort and ability, as I do in grading) helped me not only figure out something my students need help learning but also reassured me about my own teaching. I began this examination thinking that my plan for teaching students to think about novels through style, character, plot, and structure had not succeeded. I had been thinking that students really didn't understand the concepts we'd been working with. Rereading the journals and papers helped me see that students probably did understand at least two of the four concepts (I'm still left with the puzzle of why so few students wrote about plot or structure), but they need more help with the last step in the analytical process: presenting an argument and articulating connections.

Students' Perspectives on Their Learning

Students can be a great source of insight into their own learning. After all, if we want to know how well students understand literature, why not just ask them? Interviews, questionnaires, and prompts for reflective writing give students the opportunity to comment on both what they understand and what has helped them learn. They can also tell us about their reading, analysis, and writing processes. The problem is that students are not always the best judges of their own learning. Their responses to a survey or interview question about how well they understand something will tell me their perception of their learning, but a look at the work they produced may tell a different story. I learned this well in my first project. In surveys and interviews, students overwhelmingly indicated that they felt confident about their understanding of the idea of contextualizing. Their papers showed that while they may have understood the concept in general terms, they had difficulty constructing a contextual analysis. They may well have had a clear sense of the concept, but they did not have adequate strategic knowledge. This taught me never to interpret students' learning solely on the basis of their self-evaluations. Instead, I use interviews to learn about how students approach literary analysis and how they perceive the core ideas of a course. I use questionnaires to solicit students' attitudes about assignments, and I use test-like questions that ask them to demonstrate rather than comment on their learning. I also use reflective writing prompts that ask them to describe their learning experiences and display their metacognitive abilities.

Interviews

While few literary scholars use interviewing as a research tool, interviews are enjoyable and, with a little practice and strategy, fairly easy to do. After all, an interview is nothing more than a (usually recorded) conversation, albeit one in which we ask all the questions. I've conducted interviews with both individuals (students and faculty) and small groups, a technique that social scientists call focus groups. In general, I've found that interviews work best when the conversation centers on something concrete, such as a specific paper or element of a course. In examining how students learn to do interdisciplinary contextual analysis, for example, I conducted a series of individual interviews with three students, asking them about specific assignments and about their developing understanding of interdisciplinarity and contextualization. I also did a focus group session with students in a colleague's interdisciplinary course, asking them about these concepts and about what kinds of work they'd done in the course. In research for this book, I asked several faculty members to describe and comment on their own research and to discuss how their approaches emerge in their teaching. I also asked students about what they had learned as English majors, how they approached writing a research paper, what they saw as most difficult about studying literature, and how their own reading, critical thinking, and writing habits had changed over time.

A few general principles guide me whenever I'm planning and conducting interviews. One obvious concern: whom should I interview? Which students or colleagues might have a useful perspective to help me explore the issue at hand? Interviewing students raises another question: when should I conduct the interview? The best time to find out how students approached a particular assignment would be right after they had completed the paper, preferably even before I had returned it with a grade, so that the experience of writing it would be fresh in the students' minds and so their responses would not be shaded by my comments. But conducting interviews in the middle of a course can be problematic. Time is often tight during the semester, and students may feel uncomfortable revealing their thoughts to the person who controls the grade book. Given those concerns, I usually wait until after the term is over to set up the interviews. Both options have merits, and, as researchers, we need to be thoughtful about the implications of our choices.

In the interview itself, I usually try to begin with something that I think the interviewee will feel comfortable talking about. In asking students about their experiences as English majors, I began by asking why they'd chosen this major. In asking colleagues about their teaching, I began by asking about their current research. Most people are uncomfortable being interviewed, in part because an interview isn't balanced—the person being interviewed does most of the talking, which can feel like a violation of the conventions of conversation. People are often self-conscious at the beginning, because they know you're looking for something, though they aren't sure what. Many of my students and colleagues have begun by saying that they're not sure they can really tell me anything useful. I take that as an expression of concern about what the interview will cover and whether their answers will be "good enough." On the other hand, almost everyone enjoys talking about themselves, so starting with questions that invite people to do this in a relatively innocuous way can help them relax and get used to being the one doing most of the talking.

Be prepared to ask the same question several times, though in different ways. For example, in interviews about writing papers, students often gloss over the parts that I find most significant. For example, one student described her process of writing a paper this way: "I do most of my writing in my head. I don't make an outline. I don't really even take notes. I just put it together in my mind and then, I sit down and that's it." I had to ask a series of follow-up questions to encourage her to talk about how she determines the thesis or focus of a paper, how she locates and selects outside sources, and so on. Her initial response was typical. Few of us think critically or even consciously about our thinking processes. Students, especially, may give shorthand answers because they worry about giving a wrong answer and revealing that they are doing things incorrectly. Getting them to say more requires patience, but I find that just asking people to tell me more often elicits more complete responses.

Sometimes, asking about what we really want to know simply won't work. Asking a colleague about his teaching philosophy might well yield abstract and idealistic comments that don't represent how the individual actually teaches, for example. Instead, I approach some topics indirectly by posing questions that will generate answers that demonstrate how someone thinks. For example, I asked several colleagues to describe specific courses and to explain their goals and experiences. I wasn't really interested in the specific courses; rather, I wanted to find out what kinds of issues and choices faculty members make as they think about teaching. The concrete question generated responses that helped me understand my colleagues' ideas about and attitudes toward teaching, though they didn't provide that information directly.

One of the side benefits of interviewing is that it allows us to quote from students and colleagues, and their words can be powerful and engaging. In order to do that accurately, and in order to review what was said, you'll want to record the interviews. I use a small digital recorder because it is unobtrusive and doesn't create technical interruptions like the need to turn over a tape. Better yet, I can download the file onto my computer, and easily stop and start as I listen to the interview and take notes. I rarely transcribe every word of an interview, but I do take detailed notes, and I transcribe quotes that seem especially relevant or interesting. Even if you don't take notes or transcribe, listening to an interview again works much like reading a paper again: we hear things that we might have missed while conducting the interview.

I use focus groups rarely, because I find that small-group interviews usually provide less in-depth information than one-on-one conversations. On the other hand, the benefit of a small-group conversation is that individuals can clarify and contradict each other's views, and often one person will raise an idea that generates response from others. Of course, that very effect can be problematic. While interaction can generate more active responses, a single dominant individual can shape the direction of an entire conversation. But while I rarely use small-group conversations in my research, I often use them as a tool for course evaluation and informal assessment. I ask a trusted colleague to lead a discussion with my class, in my absence, about what is working, what difficulties students are having, and what they'd like to see change. These conversations are not recorded, in order to protect students' anonymity, but my colleague will synthesize students' comments and report back to me. At the next class meeting, I acknowledge students' concerns and let them know what changes I will make in response. This lets them know that I am interested not only in their perspectives but in making the course work well. This process often draws my attention to strengths and problems in the course so that I can reinforce or address them.

Questionnaires and Reflections

I have been using informal surveys and questionnaires in my classes for years. While some are part of research projects, I use others to help me evaluate the course as it progresses (see Appendix 1 for several examples). Tom Angelo and Patricia Cross call these "classroom assessment techniques."[3] They're short, informal writing prompts that ask students to reflect on what they've learned. For example, when students turn in an assignment, I might ask them to complete a separate short survey and comment on how challenging the assignment was, how well prepared they felt to complete it, and what they wish we'd spent more time on. Sometimes, I simply ask students to write at the end of class about what they found most useful and what they'd like us to discuss further. Longer, more formal questionnaires as well as prompts for self-evaluation and reflection give me insight into both how well students understand course concepts and their experiences as learners.

I use questionnaires in part because, unlike standard faculty evaluation forms (at least at my institution), they allow me to ask questions that are specific to my course. Indeed, these questionnaires usually focus on specific aspects of the course. For example, in an end-of-term survey, I might ask which assignment they found most difficult, what concept they see as most useful, or what was the most important thing they learned in the course. Students' responses help me think about what did and did not work. For example, at the end of the course in which I first used the reading journal assignment, I wasn't sure if the journal was worth doing again. But when a clear majority of students in the end-of-term survey indicated that it was the most useful assignment in the course, I thought again. I don't, on the other hand, always go along with student preferences. While many students report that they appreciate and enjoy the series of short assignments that makes up the inquiry project, some always complain that it's too much work. My response is not to drop an assignment sequence that I believe works; rather, that complaint tells me that I need to let students know that I understand their workload issues and be a little flexible on deadlines.

I also try to pose questions that, like my indirect interview questions, ask students to demonstrate their thinking. Often, these questionnaires look like exams, though I never use them as the basis for a grade. I might ask them to define key terms or to describe how they would approach a problem. While these "ungraded exams" have the same limitations of more formal tests—a limited time frame, limited space, writing by hand (which in this technological age feels increasingly awkward)—I also find their responses to questions like these especially useful. They help me identify patterns of understanding and misunderstanding. If at midterm I discover that most students can't clearly define a term or concept that's central to the course, I know I have to take more time with that idea. Like a regular exam, these questionnaires demonstrate individual students' learning, but they can also indicate what concepts or strategies need more attention in the course.

These questionnaires also can help me understand how students think about literature and literary analysis in more general terms. In researching this book, I distributed questionnaires to both faculty and students. Some parts of the questionnaires were identical, and the different patterns of response were helpful. For example, I asked students in a general education course, seniors in an English capstone course, and literature faculty to rank a set of six possible strategies for analyzing a text:

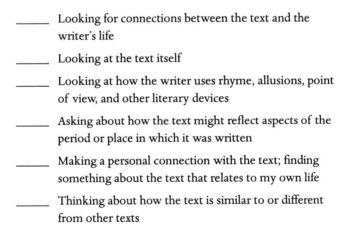

    _____ Looking for connections between the text and the writer's life

    _____ Looking at the text itself

    _____ Looking at how the writer uses rhyme, allusions, point of view, and other literary devices

    _____ Asking about how the text might reflect aspects of the period or place in which it was written

    _____ Making a personal connection with the text; finding something about the text that relates to my own life

    _____ Thinking about how the text is similar to or different from other texts

Faculty and seniors agreed that the most useful strategies were looking at the text itself and looking at how the text reflected its context, while most of the beginning students selected making a personal connection with the text. This suggests that English majors are learning to value both textual and contextual analysis while the general education students' focus on personal connection reflects the emphasis on reader response in secondary English education. On the other hand, faculty members and the seniors differed on the value of analyzing literary devices, such as allusion or point of view. For faculty, it ranked third, while students ranked it fifth. Together, these responses may suggest that we are doing a good job of teaching students to read literature contextually, but we may not be doing as well in teaching them why the form or style of a text matters.

I also use reflective writing prompts to explore students' perspectives and experiences, as well as to measure their ability to step outside of the process and think critically about their own thinking. One of my favorite end-of-term prompts asks students to chronicle briefly where they started and what happened to change their views.[4] I ask them to begin by completing a sentence beginning with "At first": "At first I hated this novel," one might write, or "At first I felt overwhelmed by the many different pieces that made up this project," or "At first I thought I knew exactly what I thought about this book." Then, I ask them to write as many "And then" statements as they wish: "And then I started looking more closely at the writer's style," or "And then I talked with Dan about his project," or "And then I started reading the critical articles." I like how this prompt invites students to reflect on how their work and thinking have changed and to tie those changes to specific moments in the course or in their individual research. I also use simpler prompts, such as asking students to write about a paper before they turn it in, identifying what they are most satisfied with and what they have struggled with.

While interviews, questionnaires, and reflective prompts give me different types of responses, all provide useful information about how students view the content, processes, and teaching approaches of my courses. They also help me include students' voices in writing about their learning. Their self-evaluations may not always be accurate, but their experiences and ideas are often both relevant and insightful.

Other Sources

None of us would write a scholarly article without reading what other critics have to say. Indeed, much of our work begins as a response to other critics' ideas. We're less likely to do this, I fear, when we examine students' learning. Not only do few of us keep up with the critical conversations in our discipline about how to teach literature, we also don't tend to read what scholars outside of our field have to say. I don't mean to suggest that we should all be reading articles on pedagogy all the time. But when I'm wrestling with a problem in my classroom, such work is invaluable. My advice on using other scholars' work in studying your students' learning is short and simple: look beyond the familiar and keep an open mind. You may find the most useful ideas come from sources that focus on a very different part of the educational landscape.

Within literary studies, a number of people have analyzed literary learning on the college level. A rash of books appeared in the late '80s and early '90s reflecting significant changes in the discipline at the time, such as the expansion of the canon, the increasing centrality of theory, and greater awareness of the diversity of our students. Scholars such as Robert Scholes, Kathleen Yancey, David Bleich, and Sheridan Blau have written books that integrate theories and concepts from literary studies with educational research to suggest interpretive models and explanations that can help us make sense of our own students' learning. As John V. Knapp suggests, we also have much to learn from our K-12 colleagues, who have developed an extensive body of critical literature about students' learning in English courses, as have scholars in education and cognitive psychology. We also have much to learn from our colleagues who specialize in writing. Not only have scholars of composition and rhetoric been doing this kind of research for decades, but many of the issues they focus on are relevant to students' learning in literature courses. Ideas about process, the relationship between personal response and academic thinking, insight into the sources and potential cures for patterns of error, and more can be gleaned from research in composition.

Several journals regularly publish articles about teaching. Many journals in composition and rhetoric provide theoretical and practical ideas, often based on classroom research. In addition, *College English* and *Pedagogy* emphasize teaching, though in both cases, as with the composition journals, most pieces look at the teaching of writing. Some more traditional literary journals, such as *Style, New Literary History,* and others, publish occasional pieces about pedagogy. The British journal *Arts and Humanities in Higher Education* focuses on the nature of knowledge and on issues of teaching in these fields. You'll find these using the standard research tools in the field, including the *MLA Bibliography*. A more general search tool, or one focused on education, will yield articles on the teaching of English on the secondary level, many of which will be relevant to college teaching.

Sources from other disciplines can be surprisingly useful, even when they focus on teaching a very different subject. I've learned from articles, websites, and books on teaching history, psychology, mathematics, sociology, biology, and many other fields, as well as from a variety of materials by education specialists, whose work may or may not focus on teaching in a specific discipline. A few journals publish articles about teaching from across the disciplines, such as *Radical Teacher, College Teaching,* and a variety of journals focused on particular issues—classroom technology, collaborative learning, and so on. In the twenty-first century, several new online journals began to focus on the scholarship of teaching and learning, such as *MountainRise* and the *Journal of the Scholarship of Teaching and Learning*. Many fields have journals that focus on teaching, and education journals, of course, publish articles on pedagogy. The key to finding these sources is determining the language used by scholars and by databases to describe the phenomenon or issue in which you're interested. Because I know that useful articles are likely to be listed under subject terms and keywords that are different from what I use, I often begin searching for relevant information by using a database that provides abstracts or allows full-text searching. That often allows me to locate a few examples, and database records will show me the "official" terms to use to find more.

Another useful strategy is simply talking with colleagues from other fields. On many campuses, multidisciplinary groups of faculty work in learning circles, reading groups, or other informal groupings to discuss ideas about teaching, consider pedagogical models, and develop effective strategies for addressing shared problems. One of my SoTL colleagues, the mathematician Anita Salem, asked Renee Michael, a colleague in the psychology department, to work with her on a project, because she knew that Michael's expertise in cognitive psychology would provide useful insights into her students' learning about calculus. At YSU, an interdisciplinary team of faculty from English and history worked together over several years to develop effective strategies for helping students learn to read primary texts. While I value scholarly sources, much of what I've learned about teaching and learning has come through these kinds of cross-disciplinary conversations.

Reading this kind of work and talking with colleagues provide me with theoretical models for explaining and understanding my students' work. These models can provide a vocabulary and rationale for analyzing students' learning and my own teaching. This often requires a kind of translation, or at least the patience to read past details that seem irrelevant to my situation. For example, I've found it useful to translate Wineburg's studies of how historians think into an exploration of how literary scholars think, and much of the work I draw upon about cognitive apprenticeship and ideas about expertise focuses on K-12 education. You may not find sources that directly address your classroom concerns, but often an article about a very different type of course will prove surprisingly useful. With some patience and intellectual openness, you may find that scholars talking about teaching in very different contexts have insights that can point you toward conceptual models, classroom strategies, and research techniques that you can use in analyzing your own students' learning.

You can also find more information about how to conduct research on students' learning online and in relevant books. A good starting place for online resources is the International Society for the Scholarship of Teaching and Learning (www.issotl.org), which has links to online tutorials, resource collections, and examples. As part of its ten-year initiative to foster SoTL work on campuses around the country, the Carnegie Foundation for the Advancement of Teaching developed several books, including *Opening Lines: Approaches to the Scholarship of Teaching and Learning* (edited by Pat Hutchings), *Disciplinary Styles in the Scholarship of Teaching and Learning: Exploring Common Ground* (edited by Mary Taylor Huber and Sherwyn P. Morreale), and *The Advancement of Learning: Building the Teaching Commons* (edited by Huber and Hutchings).

A Few Words on Ethics

The research we do on our students' learning may affect them in multiple ways. While it can help us develop more effective teaching methods and give us insight into our students' perspectives, it can also create discomfort and even, in some cases, risk for students. This is especially true when we use students' work and their words in articles, presentations, and books. Given that the scholarship of teaching and learning often focuses not on successes but on difficulties, we're likely to want to focus on how students get things wrong. Doing so exposes our struggles, but it also exposes our students.

I learned this early in my SoTL work when I gave a presentation to a group of colleagues in the Visible Knowledge Project, using video clips of an interview with a couple of students. Their reflections on their experiences working with a particular website generated laughter among my colleagues, in part because my students were being deliberately funny, but also because their comments revealed their lack of understanding and the limits of their life experience. Because they were, in part, performing for the camera, some of the laughter was appropriate, but not all. While the students weren't present, I knew that they would have felt embarrassed and uncomfortable had they been in the room. I felt bad for them but also foolish, because I hadn't considered how the video might work in that setting. Before that moment, I had brushed aside the concerns raised by colleagues in other fields about the ethics of studying students' learning. I simply refused to believe that anything I could do would cause my students harm. The experience with the video taught me to be more protective of my students and more cautious about how I use evidence, especially when it's evidence that showcases their limitations.

As professionals, we have a responsibility to treat our students respectfully and to be thoughtful about how we collect and present information about our students. As a teacher, I believe, I have the right to review my students' work and to administer informal classroom assessments without asking their permission, as long as I don't share that information with anyone else. As a scholar, however, I have a responsibility to protect the interests of the subjects of my research, especially when I present students' work to colleagues or make it public. I do that in two ways. First, I ask students to sign a form giving me permission to analyze and quote from their work (see Appendix 2 for an example). I usually don't distribute this until the end of the term, in part because I often don't know that I want to study a course until that point. But I also worry that if I let students know earlier in the course that I am studying them, they will feel self-conscious. I honestly don't know whether that would make a real difference, but I don't think there's a benefit to making my research an issue until it needs to be. Second, I use students' work anonymously, unless they specifically request that I use their real names (as a few students always do). In this book, for example, I've assigned pseudonyms to most of the students. I also make an effort to describe students' work generously; I always try to imagine how the students would feel about reading my discussion of their work.

Concern about the fair use and legal control of students' work has grown since the 1990s. On most campuses, faculty who engage in SoTL must submit proposals to the institutional review board (IRB), asking permission to collect and analyze student papers, conduct interviews, or distribute surveys. Some journals and publishers now require scholars to get permission from the students we quote for specific uses of their material. When I published an article in one journal, for example, I had to send each student a letter with the passage in which I used their words, asking for permission to quote them in that way. While I understand the concern for students' rights, I also know that this kind of requirement discourages faculty—especially those of us in the humanities who never even knew that IRBs existed—from pursuing this kind of research. Producing IRB proposals for work on education may be unfamiliar to us, and the very idea may feel intimidating, but they are not difficult to write (see Appendix 3 for an example).

Underlying all of this bureaucracy is an important core idea: we have an ethical responsibility not just to think critically about how well our pedagogy works and to teach as well as we can but also to treat students and their work with respect. We should, I believe, operate on the assumption that most of our students are making an effort and that we hold some responsibility for any difficulties they experience. We must also take responsibility for protecting students' interests and reputations. This need not create significant obstacles. It just takes a little extra attention.

The "A" Word

Assessment has become a dirty word on many college campuses, and this may be especially true in the humanities, because we perceive the demands that we define concrete learning outcomes and measurable evidence as running counter to some of our core values. As I have written elsewhere, faculty have good reasons to be wary about assessment. We also have good reasons to take it seriously.[5] If we want to resist moves toward standardization, an overreliance on quantitative data, and an excessive emphasis on preparing students for the workplace, one effective strategy is to offer alternative models that use methods and emphasize values that reflect our disciplinary perspective. For many English departments, the question of "measuring student learning outcomes," to use the language of the assessment movement, creates anxiety, because we don't think of ourselves as scholars who "measure" anything, and we see much of what we teach as poorly suited to measurement at all. SoTL strategies can help us develop a more interpretive approach, one that generates useful insights into student learning while also using discipline-appropriate methods. While it might seem easiest to accept standardized tests, such as the English Major Field Test developed by the Educational Testing Service,[6] because they do the work for us and produce the quantitative results that some campus assessment offices demand, I suggest that we instead adapt the methods I've discussed here—methods that are, to a great extent, based in our disciplinary practices—to program assessment.

We can use all of the methods I've described above to assess students' learning in a program, just as we can use those methods to analyze their learning in a particular course. But doing so requires two important shifts. The first is that assessment on this level is inherently collaborative, because its focus is not on a single course but on a whole program. Even if only a few faculty members take responsibility for assessment, they must coordinate their efforts, and they must consider the full range of courses that make up the major. In most cases, this means working together to identify learning outcomes or goals. Just as I suggested we do in planning courses, assessment encourages departments to use backward design, to begin by defining where students will be at the end. This in itself is a challenge, because we don't usually engage in that kind of discussion. Assessment also requires collaboration in order to decide what evidence of student learning to examine and how to evaluate it.

The second shift that is necessary in adapting SoTL for assessment is to move away from a focus on problems and toward a focus on evaluation. Instead of asking "What works?" or "Why doesn't this work?" an assessment asks, "How well does this work?" No doubt, some faculty may worry that an assessment will reveal significant problems with their programs, and having problems with a program is a much more troubling concern than having problems with a specific assignment or with teaching a particular concept. While I would argue that identifying problems is worthwhile, because that is the first step toward improving a program, departments often feel pressure to use an assessment to demonstrate that their programs are effective. For most departments, asking "How well does our major work?" will yield evidence of success even as it may reveal a few challenges. Ironically, it's when faculty are willing to recognize those challenges that the value of assessment becomes clear. When assessment helps us make our programs better, which it does in part by helping us understand both what works and what is not working so well, then the time and effort it takes are worth investing. When assessment helps us solve problems, it serves our interests and the interests of our students, not just the interests of the institution or external evaluators.

Adapting SoTL to program assessment will require different strategies for collecting materials to analyze. Just as we have to select the most useful materials when we want to study an issue in our own courses and we have to figure out how to collect that data, department assessment committees must determine which materials they want to review and develop strategies for collecting them. One of the most common ways of doing this is the student portfolio. A number of English departments ask students to assemble sets of papers and projects representing their experience in the major and demonstrating their learning. Often, these papers are accompanied with reflective writing in which students identify their individual strengths and challenges, significant learning experiences, goals, and/or questions. Other departments, instead of asking students to select from their own work, collect papers from specific courses, often an entry-level Introduction to Literary Studies and a senior-level course, especially a capstone.

SoTL provides us with tools for assessing portfolios or collections of sample papers. As I discussed above, reading student work attentively, much as we do works of literature, can provide useful insights into what students have learned. At YSU, each student portfolio is read by at least one faculty member, who writes comments and discusses her observations with other members of the assessment committee. The committee as a whole reads a few of the portfolios as well, to provide a common basis for comparison and discussion. In some English departments, students and faculty meet together to discuss their portfolios.

The collective nature of assessment and the emphasis in many institutional assessment programs on quantitative data encourage us to find ways to standardize those readings. In many cases, we mistakenly assume that assessment must be quantitative because the models we're offered rely on numerical data. But even without a quantitative requirement, a program assessment usually involves multiple members of a department applying a shared set of criteria to a sample of portfolios and sample papers. Often, this means developing a rubric that identifies the qualities of a strong paper or portfolio and asking faculty to rate how well each sample achieves that ideal. Other rubrics describe different levels of performance on multiple elements. If different levels of achievement on the rubric are given numeric values, the results can be tabulated to provide quantitative data. Such numbers are not likely to prove useful to humanities faculty, but defining both the elements to include on a rubric and the qualities of strong performance can, in itself, provide faculty with insight into the department's expectations and students' work. Equally important, patterns will emerge when multiple faculty members rate students' work using the same rubric. It's useful to have everyone involved apply the rubric to a small set of materials and discuss the results, as well as to divide the materials so that no one has to read every sample paper or student portfolio.

Another strategy that can work well for English departments involves faculty examining their own students' learning and then comparing notes with their colleagues. In many departments, multiple faculty members teach variations of the same course, and by comparing notes they can develop a shared understanding of what students bring to the course, how different assignments or classroom activities work, and what difficulties students encounter. The same could be done with different courses that fulfill the same function in the major, such as surveys or courses that emphasize a particular type of writing. A written summary of these discussions can be part of a department's assessment report. This approach encourages individual faculty to engage in the kinds of critical analysis of students' learning that SoTL promotes, and it fosters both mutual understanding of and shared knowledge about teaching and learning in the department. Some faculty may resist investing the time to do this, and some may not feel comfortable sharing their insights with each other. In some departments, intellectual and personal divisions would make this approach difficult, but when it can be accomplished, even if it involves only some members of the department, students will benefit from what faculty learn from each other.

Both of these models operate on an assumption that I think many campus assessment offices accept but about which many faculty are, perhaps rightly, skeptical: the purpose of assessment is not to account for their performance to some institutional or external judge but rather to help departments serve their students well. Yes, underlying some of these external calls for assessment are suspicions that we are not doing our jobs well enough. And yes, state legislators and the U.S. Department of Education have called for greater accountability. In most cases, though, their concerns are directed toward institutional-level issues: enrollment, costs, graduation rates. It's worth noting, too, that accrediting organizations are often more interested in fostering a "culture of student learning" than they are in creating a "culture of accountability." The Higher Learning Commission, for example, sponsors an Academy for Assessment of Student Learning that emphasizes the value of multidisciplinary projects that examine questions that matter to those on a particular campus rather than standardized approaches or proving the effectiveness of programs or schools. No doubt, department-level assessment takes time, even more than the work we do examining our own courses, time for which few faculty are compensated or rewarded. We're right to resent demands that we prove that we're doing our jobs and to resist the requirement for unrewarded extra labor.

Despite the validity of these concerns, assessment is worth our attention, and we can make it fit comfortably into our discipline. Assessment can offer an opportunity to demonstrate to skeptical outsiders that we are critically engaged in our students' learning, but it can also help us discover how well we're doing and help us develop strategies for making our English programs more effective. Ideally, assessment can foster critical conversations about teaching and learning within our departments, which, in turn, can build support for individual classroom research. Indeed, while this entire book is the result of projects that engaged me as an individual and in critical conversations with my colleagues about our students' learning, it also reflects my persistent hope that the insights of many scholars of composition, literary studies, and SoTL will inspire better, more deliberate teaching about literature.

Research That Makes a Difference

Figuring out what and how students think is a challenging puzzle, one that is both intellectual and emotional, practical and theoretical. While many academics chose this profession because they love research, many others are motivated by a love of teaching. For us, the opportunity to think critically about our own pedagogical assumptions and habits, to understand more deeply how our students learn, to keep playing with strategies to facilitate learning is engaging and exciting. Such work offers many benefits. Reflecting on the nature of our own knowledge, recognizing how our content and strategic knowledge shape each other, can clarify what our students need to learn. The insights of our colleagues in education and psychology can help us to rethink how we plan courses, use class time, and interact with students. The scholarship of teaching and learning takes that engagement further, inviting us to become researchers, to dig deeper into the problems of learning about literature, and, as we adapt our strategic knowledge to the texts of student learning, to expand and develop our own analytical habits. What we learn in the process can improve our students' learning and, when we choose to make our work public, help colleagues gain insight into their own students' experiences.

All of this is, I believe, research that makes a difference. Like many humanists, I sometimes struggle to justify, even to myself, the time I devote to analyzing centuries-old and often obscure works of literature. My most widely read literary analyses make a real contribution to audiences of a few dozen or, maybe, when my work is especially significant, of a few hundred. Devoting similar attention to the teaching of literature has a more practical outcome and reaches a far larger audience. I don't mean to suggest that literary scholarship is unimportant. But it does seem worthwhile to commit some of my scholarly energies to work that will reach hundreds of students directly, helping them develop skills in critical reading and writing that they can use not only as future workers and scholars but as citizens. When such work finds an additional audience of other teachers, that effect multiplies. Good teaching can make a difference. And good teaching comes not merely from innate ability or intelligence but from critical engagement with the knowledge of our discipline, the insights of scholars who study how people learn, and the evidence of our students' learning. That kind of teaching matters.

APPENDIXES

Appendix 1.
Sample Questionnaires and Reflective Writing Prompts

Sample A: Opening-Day Survey

1. Why do people read literature?

2. Why do schools—high schools and colleges alike—require students to study literature?

3. When you read literature, what do you focus on?

4. Please indicate whether the following statements are true or false:

   T / F   Each poem or story has a true and correct meaning.

   T / F   The real meaning of a literary text is what the author intended it to mean.

   T / F   Every reader creates his/her own meaning for a poem or story.

   T / F   All interpretations of a story or poem are equally valid.

   T / F   A story or poem may have several different meanings.

   T / F   Some interpretations of a poem or story can be completely wrong.

   T / F   Expert readers see things in texts that I don't notice.

   T / F   Expert readers come to new texts with a lot of background knowledge that helps them make sense of what the story or poem means.

5. Which of the following best describes how you develop an interpretation of a story or poem? (Check only one)

_____ I usually figure out what I think it means right away, and then look for evidence to support my interpretation.

_____ I have to think about different ways of interpreting it before I decide what it means.

_____ I try to figure out the single best interpretation of a poem or story.

_____ I like to hear what other people think before developing my own interpretation.

_____ I like to consider several possible meanings instead of trying to settle on just one.

6. How do you figure out the meaning of a story or poem? Rank the following strategies in order of which you find most useful (1) to least useful (6).

_____ Knowing something about the writer and his/her life

_____ Looking at the text itself

_____ Looking at how the writer uses rhyme, genre, allusions, irony, or other literary devices

_____ Knowing about the issues in society at the time when it was written

_____ Making a personal connection with the text

_____ Comparing the story or poem with others that you've read

_____ Other (describe)

Sample B: Completely UNGRADED Midterm

Please define the following terms or concepts:

Intent

Use

Memory

Signs

Structure

Cultural conversation (or culture as a conversation)

Interdisciplinary analysis

For each of these concepts, rate your level of understanding, using the following scale:

1 = I've never heard of this.

2 = I have some idea of what this is, but I don't feel comfortable defining it.

3 = I can define this, but I still feel somewhat confused about it.

4 = I feel fairly confident that I understand this, but I have a few questions.

5 = I understand this very well.

Write your rating in the left-hand margin beside each item.

Imagine that I've assigned you to write a paper analyzing how the experience of work changed in Youngstown after the mills shut down around 1980. How would you use interdisciplinary approaches to complete this assignment?

As you worked on the text analysis, text web, and reading-texts-through-history papers, what difficulties or confusions did you encounter?

How well do you think you resolved those difficulties?

What are you still confused about?

What do you think was the greatest strength of your work on the first three projects?

What would you like to learn about during the second half of this course that we haven't yet fully explored?

Which of the following experiences related to this course has most helped you learn? Note: I'm *not* asking which you most enjoyed, but which contributed the most to your understanding.

_____ Readings

_____ Lectures

_____ Full-class discussions

_____ Small-group discussions

_____ Computer lab activities

_____ Materials on the course website

_____ Completing the assignments

_____ Talking with other students outside of class

_____ Talking with the instructor outside of class

_____ Reflecting on course material on my own

What should we do more of during the second half of the semester?

Write your own explanation of each of the following ideas:

In American culture, and specifically in the Youngstown area, work and class help to form individual and community identity but are also sources of conflict within the community.

Literature exists within a cultural framework, not as something separate from its culture but rather as a set of texts that are intimately involved with culture.

Interdisciplinary analysis can yield rich, complex insights into representations, including literary texts, and into the processes of identity formation, cultural negotiation, and social change.

Appendix 2. Sample Consent Letter

Dear Student,

I am conducting a study to explore students' experiences in general education literature courses. The study involves three elements:

- two in-class diagnostic exercises, one at the beginning of the semester and one at the end;
- a series of videotaped small-group conversations with a few volunteers from the class;
- collecting copies of students' work.

I will analyze these materials, after the course is over, and use what I learn to improve the way I teach this course.

Your participation in this study does not put you at risk in any way. The diagnostic exercises will not affect your grade in any way. I will not view the videotapes of the small-group conversations until after the semester is over and final grades have been filed. Any quotations or paraphrases of your work will be presented anonymously in research publications or presentations based on this course.

Your participation in this study is completely voluntary, and you may withdraw at any time without any consequences. Your decisions about whether and how to participate will not affect your course grade.

If you have any questions, please feel free to talk with me.

Thank you for your assistance.

Sincerely,
Sherry Linkon

Appendix 3. Sample IRB Proposal

Most institutional review boards define classroom research as "exempt," so an application for approval usually consists of just a simple form and an abstract describing the research. Here is a sample IRB abstract:

> Many faculty members have become interested in how students in general education and introductory courses approach reading assignments, especially those in literature in which they must use a variety of strategies to determine meaning. It seems clear that when students have become engaged in a work of literature, they are more likely to read it carefully and to think about it effectively and productively. But what engages students in literary assignments, and how can we facilitate that engagement? In pursuing this question, we became aware that there is a significant difference between the strategies—that is, the methods, tools, intuitions, and experience—that we in the discipline bring to our reading of literature and the ways that our students approach the same works.
>
> Although little research has been done in this area to date, a preliminary study on how learning occurs (April 1999), conducted by the NRC Committee on Developments in the Science of Learning, and a study carrying that work forward by a second NRC committee, the Committee on Learning Research and Educational Practice (Bransford et al. 1999), explore the differences in the ways experts and novices perceive and understand the same stimulus and conclude that "effective instruction begins with the knowledge and skills that learners bring to the learning task." We need a greater understanding of our students' reading strategies so that we can more effectively integrate that understanding into our teaching and learn about how engagement comes about. The study we propose aims to explore the relationship between the ways our students approach literary reading assignments and their engagement in those readings.
>
> Our mode of analysis will be qualitative, consisting of close readings of students' written responses to a variety of texts. We propose to gather data from students in a number of Introduction to Literature classes at Youngstown State University (English 1590, Spring 2005). This is a general education course with no prerequi-

sites, so we will be looking at students who are most likely freshmen and who have not yet had any college literature courses. We
will construct brief writing assignments that ask them to demonstrate and explore their own reading and thinking habits when
they approach a new piece of literature. We will also interview
students in focus groups (six–eight students) to hear their perspectives on the question of how they enter into assigned literary readings and what strategies they bring to the task.

This is an initial exploration that will help us to develop better
questions and more effective assessment tools for discovering how
our students actually enter into literary texts. Our findings may
lead us to a clearer understanding of how we might develop more
effective methods of helping our students become better readers
of literature. This study participates in the scholarship of teaching
and learning and not only should inform our teaching, but should
generate further research projects that will result in publishable
findings.

NOTES

1. The Literary Mind

1. Steven Mailloux provides a useful overview of the history of reader-response criticism and pedagogy in "The Turns of Reader-Response Criticism."

2. See, for example, Maria-Regina Kecht's *Pedagogy Is Politics*, James F. Slevin and Art Young's *Critical Theory and the Teaching of Literature*, James Engell and David Perkins's *Teaching Literature*, as well as multidisciplinary books on feminist pedagogy, such as *Gender and Academe*, edited by Sara Munson Deats and Lagretta Tallent Lenker, and multiculturalism, such as *Between Borders*, edited by Henry A. Giroux and Peter McLaren.

3. See chapter 2 of Bransford et al., *How People Learn*, "How Experts Differ from Novices," for a fuller explanation and examples of these concepts.

4. This concept was developed with Russian scholar Melissa Smith, English professor Stephanie Tingley, and historian Martha Pallante, in conversations as a campus team in the Visible Knowledge Project.

5. To preserve anonymity, I provide no specific citations for quotes from interviews with students and colleagues. I gave each person the option of being referred to here by their real name or a pseudonym.

6. I surveyed forty-seven literature faculty members from fourteen institutions around the United States. The survey is available online, http://www.surveymonkey.com/s.aspx?sm=eUdOaPRg4QOUkIwIh7q79w_3d_3d.

7. Mariolina Salvatori and Pat Donohue have written an excellent textbook, *The Elements (and Pleasures) of Difficulty*, that guides students through the uses of difficulty, illustrating clearly the idea that difficulty is a useful starting place, not a sign of trouble. Similarly, in his book *The Literature Workshop*, Sheridan Blau encourages literature teachers to focus on the least-clear rather than the best-understood parts of texts. As both books show, difficulty can be productive in the classroom as well as for literary scholarship.

8. Wineburg made extensive use of think-alouds in his research on historical thinking. He describes the technique fully in chapter 3 of *Historical Thinking and Other Unnatural Acts*.

9. Bass explored this concept in a research project with students in a course called Reading the U.S. Cultural Past, which he reported in a "poster" on the Visible Knowledge Project website. Although much of the content of his poster is no longer available, the rough outline of Bass's study can be seen on the VKP site.

10. The concept of a rhetorical vocabulary developed through an e-mail conversation with Randy Bass and Michael Coventry about the challenge of preparing students to read theoretical texts.

2. Making Literary Thinking Visible

1. I discuss this project in some depth, with examples of students' work, in my online course portfolio, *Learning Interdisciplinarity*, http://gallery.carnegiefoundation .org/collections/castl_he/slinkon/CoursePortfolioHome.htm.

2. The "Alien Song" video can be found on YouTube, http://www.you tube.com/results?search_query=alien+song&search=Search.

3. While I have adapted it over time, I began with a style sheet created by Lakeside School teacher Erik Christensen, which is available online, http://www.lake sideschool.org/upperschool/departments/english/ErikChristensen/WRITING%20 STRATEGIES/LiteraryStyles.htm.

4. For a useful introduction to this concept, see "Decoding the Disciplines," by Joan Middendorf and David Pace.

3. Course Design for Literary Learning

1. The chapter "Learning and Transfer," in Bransford et al.'s *How People Learn* provides a useful overview of this research.

2. These examples are paraphrased from actual assignments that I found online.

3. I am grateful to Rina Benmayor, from California State University, Monterey Bay, who suggested this strategy after reading some of my students' papers and noting that students seemed to lose their engagement and confidence when they moved from informal to formal writing.

4. An earlier version of this discussion of the inquiry project appeared in Linkon, "The Reader's Apprentice."

4. Analyzing Students' Learning

1. For a good example of the effective integration of students' work, a discussion of the local context, and the application of theoretical models, see Salibrici and Salter, "The Transitional Space of Hidden Writing."

2. A description of Sandefur's project is available online, http://www1.george town.edu/college/research/45589.html.

3. Angelo and Cross have published an extensive collection of these in *Classroom Assessment Techniques*. Along with providing samples, the book also suggests how the different strategies can be used and adapted. For teachers who are just beginning to examine their students' learning, this book provides concrete and easy-to-use examples.

4. I learned this technique from Rabbi Jeffrey Schein, a professor at the Siegal College of Judaic Studies in Cleveland, who credits psychologist Ira Progoff's *Intensive Journal* program.

5. See Linkon, "How Can Assessment Work for Us?"

6. For more information on this test, visit the ETS website, www.ets.org.

BIBLIOGRAPHY

Angelo, Thomas A., and K. Patricia Cross. *Classroom Assessment Techniques: A Handbook for College Teachers*. San Francisco: Jossey-Bass, 1993.

Bass, Randy. "The Scholarship of Teaching and Learning: What's the Problem?" *Inventio*. Feb. 1999. http://www.doiiit.gmu.edu/Archives/feb98/randybass.htm.

———. "An Inquiry into Student Reading Practices in a 19th-Century American Literature Course." Poster, Visible Knowledge Project, 2002. http://cndls .georgetown.edu/lumen/vkp/profiles/dsp_posters.cfm. 6 July 2009.

Bass, Randy, and Bret Eynon. "Capturing the Visible Evidence of Invisible Learning" (Part II). *Academic Commons*. 7 Jan. 2009. http://www.academiccommons.org/ commons/essay/capturing-visible-evidence-invisible-learning-2. 25 July 2009.

Bass, Randy, and Sherry Lee Linkon. "On the Evidence of Theory: Close Reading as a Disciplinary Model for Writing about Teaching and Learning." *Arts and Humanities in Higher Education* 7 (2008): 245–261.

Bialostosky, Don. "What Should College English Be? Should College English Be Close Reading?" *College English* 69.2 (Nov. 2006): 111–116.

Blau, Sheridan D. *The Literature Workshop: Teaching Texts and Their Readers*. Portsmouth, N.H.: Heinemann, 2003.

Bleich, David. *Readings and Feelings: An Introduction to Subjective Criticism*. Urbana, Ill.: National Council of Teachers of English, 1975.

———. *Subjective Criticism*. Baltimore: Johns Hopkins University Press, 1978.

Bransford, John D., Ann L. Brown, and Rodney R. Cocking. *How People Learn: Brain, Mind, Experience, and School*. Washington, D.C.: National Academy Press, 1999.

Brubaker, Rogers. "Social Theory as Habitus." In Craig Calhoun, Edward LiPuma, and Moishe Postone, eds., *Bourdieu: Critical Perspectives*. Chicago: University of Chicago Press, 1993. 212–234.

Calder, Lendol, and Sarah-Eva Carlson. "Using 'Think Alouds' to Evaluate Deep Understanding." 2002. http://www.uc.edu/cetl/documents/thinkalouds.pdf. 26 July 2009.

Carnochan, W. B. "The English Curriculum: Past and Present." *PMLA: Publications of the Modern Language Association of America* 115.7 (Dec. 2000): 1958–1960.

Carter, Michael. "The Idea of Expertise: An Exploration of Cognitive and Social Dimensions of Writing." *College Composition and Communication* 41 (Oct. 1990): 265–286.

Chick, Nancy. "Unpacking a Signature Pedagogy in Literary Studies." In Regar A. R. Guring, Nancy Chick, and Aeron Haynie, eds., *Exploring Signature Pedagogies: Approaches to Teaching Disciplinary Habits of Mind*. Sterling, Va.: Stylus, 2008.

Collins, Allan, John Seely Brown, and Ann Holum. "Cognitive Apprenticeship: Making Thinking Visible." *The 21st Century Learning Initiative*. http://www .211earn.org/archive/articles/brown_seely.php. 24 Nov. 2008. Reprinted from *American Educator* (Winter 1991).

Collins, Allan, John Seely Brown, and Susan E. Newman. "Cognitive Apprenticeship: Teaching the Crafts of Reading, Writing, and Mathematics." In L. B. Resnick, ed., *Knowing, Learning, and Instruction: Essays in Honor of Robert Glaser*. Hillsdale, N.J.: Erlbaum, 1989. 453–494.

Cromwell, Lucy. "Reading and Responding to Literature: Developing Critical Perspectives." In Tim Riordan and James Roth, eds., *Disciplines as Frameworks for Student Learning: Teaching the Practice of the Disciplines*. Sterling, Va.: Stylus, 2005. 77–93.

Deats, Sara Munson, and Lagretta Tallent Lenker, eds. *Gender and Academe: Feminist Pedagogy and Politics*. Lanham, Md.: Rowman & Littlefield, 1994.

Department of English Literature. Swarthmore College. http://www.swarthmore .edu/englishliterature.xml. 11 Sept. 2008.

Donald, Janet Gail. *Learning to Think: Disciplinary Perspectives*. San Francisco: Jossey-Bass, 2002.

DuBois, Andrew. "Close Reading: An Introduction." In Frank Lentricchia and Andrew DuBois, eds., *Close Reading: The Reader*. Durham, N.C.: Duke University Press, 2003.

Elliott, Michael A., and Claudia Stokes. "Introduction: What Is Method and Why Does It Matter?" In Michael A. Elliott and Claudia Stokes, eds., *American Literary Studies: A Methodological Reader*. New York: New York University Press, 2003. 1–15.

Emig, Janet. "Our Missing Theory." In Charles Moran and Elizabeth F. Penfield, eds., *Conversations: Contemporary Critical Theory and the Teaching of Literature*. Urbana, Ill.: NCTE Press, 1990. 87–96.

Empson, William. *Seven Types of Ambiguity*. London: Chatto and Windus, 1930.

Engell, James, and David Perkins, eds. *Teaching Literature: What Is Needed Now*. Cambridge, Mass.: Harvard University Press, 1988.

Fister, Barbara. "Reintroducing Students to Good Research." Gustavus Adolphus College. http://homepages.gac.edu/~fister/LakeForest.html. 14 Nov. 2008.

Frye, Northrop. *The Anatomy of Criticism*. 1957. New York: Atheneum, 1966.

Gallop, Jane. "The Historicization of Literary Studies and the Fate of Close Reading." *Profession 2007*: 181–186.

Gergits, Julia, James Schramer, and Stephanie Tingley. "Question about Student Aesthetics." Poster, Visible Knowledge Project, 2006. http://cndls.georgetown .edu/lumen/vkp/profiles/dsp_posters.cfm. 7 July 2009.

Giroux, Henry A., and Peter McLaren, eds. *Between Borders: Pedagogy and the Politics of Cultural Studies*. London: Routledge, 1994.

Huber, Mary Taylor, and Pat Hutchings. *The Advancement of Learning: Building the Teaching Commons*. San Francisco: Jossey-Bass, 2005.

Huber, Mary Taylor, and Sherwyn P. Morreale, eds. *Disciplinary Styles in the Scholarship of Teaching and Learning: Exploring Common Ground*. Washington, D.C.: American Association for Higher Education; Menlo Park, Calif.: Carnegie Foundation for the Advancement of Teaching, 2002.

Hutchings, Pat, ed. *Opening Lines: Approaches to the Scholarship of Teaching and Learning*. Menlo Park, Calif.: Carnegie Foundation for the Advancement of Teaching, 2000.

Hynds, Susan. "Questions of Difficulty in Literary Reading." In Alan C. Purves, ed., *The Idea of Difficulty in Literature*. Albany: State University of New York Press, 1996. 117–139.

Kecht, Maria-Regina, ed. *Politics Is Pedagogy: Literary Theory and Critical Teaching*. Urbana: University of Illinois Press, 1992.

Knapp, John V. "Current Conversations in the Teaching of College-Level Literature." *Style* 38.1 (2004): 50–92.

Lentricchia, Frank, and Andrew DuBois, eds. *Close Reading: The Reader*. Durham N.C.: Duke University Press, 2003.

Linkon, Sherry Lee. "How Can Assessment Work for Us?" *Academe* 91 (July–Aug. 2005): 28–32.

———. "The Reader's Apprentice: Making Critical Cultural Reading Visible." *Pedagogy* 5.2 (2005): 247–273.

Mailloux, Steven. "The Turns of Reader-Response Criticism." In Charles Moran and Elizabeth F. Penfield, eds., *Conversations: Contemporary Critical Theory and the Teaching of Literature*. Urbana, Ill.: NCTE Press, 1990. 38–54.

McCormick, Kathleen. *The Culture of Reading and the Teaching of English*. Manchester, England: Manchester University Press, 1994.

Middendorf, Joan, and David Pace. "Decoding the Disciplines: A Model for Helping Students Learn Disciplinary Ways of Thinking." *New Directions for Teaching & Learning* 98 (Summer 2004): 1–12.

Miller, J. Hillis. "My Fifty Years in the Profession." *ADE Bulletin* 123 (Winter 2003): 63–66.

Moran, Charles, and Elizabeth F. Penfield, eds. *Conversations: Contemporary Critical Theory and the Teaching of Literature*. Urbana, Ill.: NCTE Press, 1990.

Progoff, Ira. *Progoff Intensive Journal Program for Self-Development*. http://www.intensivejournal.org. 24 July 2009.

Rosenblatt, Louise. *Literature as Exploration*. New York: Appleton-Century, 1938.

Salem, Anita, and Renee Michael. "Calculus Conversations: Making Student Thinking Visible." *Gallery, Carnegie Foundation for the Advancement of Teaching*. http://gallery.carnegiefoundation.org/collections/castl_he/asalem/index.htm. 23 July 2009.

Salibrici, Mary M., and Richard C. Salter. "The Transitional Space of Hidden Writing: A Resource for Teaching Critical Insight and Concern." *Pedagogy* 4.2 (2004): 215–240.

Salvatori, Mariolina. "The Scholarship of Teaching: Beyond the Anecdotal." *Pedagogy* 2.3 (Fall 2002): 297–310.

Salvatori, Mariolina, and Pat Donohue. *The Elements (and Pleasures) of Difficulty*. New York: Pearson, 2005.

Sandefur, Jim. "You Do the Math." *Center for New Designs in Learning and Scholarship*. Georgetown University. http://cndls.georgetown.edu/index.cfm?fuseaction=main.projectDetail&projectid=42. 24 July 2009.

Scholes, Robert E. *Textual Power: Literary Theory and the Teaching of English*. New Haven, Conn.: Yale University Press, 1985.

———. *Protocols of Reading*. New Haven, Conn.: Yale University Press, 1989.

————. *The Rise and Fall of English: Reconstructing English as a Discipline.* New Haven, Conn.: Yale University Press, 1998.

————. *The Crafty Reader.* New Haven, Conn.: Yale University Press, 2001.

————. "The Transition to College Reading." *Pedagogy* 2.2 (Spring 2002): 165–172.

Schwartz, Lawrence. "The Postmodern English Major: A Case Study." *ADE Bulletin* 123 (Winter 2003): 16–24.

Scott, Nathan A., Jr. "On the Teaching of Literature in an Age of Carnival." In James Engell James and David Perkins, eds., *Teaching Literature: What Is Needed Now.* Cambridge, Mass.: Harvard University Press, 1988. 49–64.

Showalter, Elaine. *Teaching Literature.* Malden, Mass.: Blackwell, 2003.

Shulman, Lee S. "Signature Pedagogies in the Professions." *Daedalus* 134.3 (Summer 2005): 52–59.

Slevin, James F., and Art Young, eds. *Critical Theory and the Teaching of Literature: Politics, Curriculum, Pedagogy.* Urbana, Ill.: NCTE Press, 1995.

Tompkins, Jane P. "Pedagogy of the Distressed." *College English* 52.6 (Oct. 1990): 53–60.

————. *A Life in School: What the Teacher Learned.* Reading, Mass.: Addison-Wesley, 1997.

"The Undergraduate Program." Department of English. Indiana University. http://www.iub.edu/~engweb/Undergraduate.php. 11 Sept. 2008.

Webster, John. "Whose Poem Is This Anyway? Teaching Spenser through the Stanza Workshop." *Pedagogy* 3.2 (Spring 2003): 197–204.

Wiggins, Grant, and Jay McTighe. *Understanding by Design.* Alexandria, Va.: Association for Supervision and Curriculum Development, 1999.

Wineburg, Sam. *Historical Thinking and Other Unnatural Acts.* Philadelphia: Temple University Press, 2001.

————. "Teaching the Mind Good Habits." *Chronicle Review* 49.31 (11 Apr. 2003): B20.

Yancey, Kathleen Blake. *Teaching Literature as Reflective Practice.* Urbana, Ill.: National Council of Teachers of English, 2004.

INDEX

Alignment, 99
Alverno College, 28
Ambiguity, 12, 86
Annotated bibliography, 90, 115
Anonymous use of students' work, 117, 121, 137, 149
Assessment
    adapting scholarship of teaching and learning strategies for, 129, 138–141
    classroom, 129, 130, 136, 154n3 (chap. 4)
    faculty resistance to, 138, 142
    in the humanities, xi, 82, 137–141
Assignments, xiv, xv, 48, 52, 70–72, 99, 100–102, 140
    students' responses to, 92–96, 117, 121, 126, 127, 130
    See also Incremental learning; *specific assignments*

Backward design, 72–79, 138
Bass, Randy, xv, 21, 35, 107, 108, 153n9
Best practices, 81
Bleich, David, 3, 9, 133
Bourdieu, Pierre, 6, 47–48, 94–95
Bransford, John, 4, 150
    on expertise, 4–6, 7, 24, 32, 37

Capstone course, 27, 131, 139
Carnegie Foundation for the Advancement of Teaching, xv, 135
Chesnutt, Charles, teaching of, 18, 53–55
Chick, Nancy, 35, 36
Christ in Concrete, teaching of, ix
Classroom assessment techniques, 130, 154n3
Close reading, xi, 16–17, 107, 110, 150
Coaching, xiv, 24, 33, 69, 71, 79, 88, 94–98, 99
Coding, 118

Cognitive apprenticeship, 38–39, 42, 43, 44, 58, 78, 79, 87, 98, 135
    See also Coaching; Modeling; Scaffolding
Complexity, xi, 9, 11, 12, 42, 44, 82, 86, 91, 118
Composition research, xiv, 71, 95, 133, 142
Consent letter, 149
Content knowledge, xiv, 2–3, 8, 41, 52, 66, 78, 142
    in course planning, 58, 59–60, 70, 71, 72, 76, 98, 99, 100–101, 103–104
    in the English major, 24, 25–28, 35, 38
    of experts, 5–6, 19, 20, 22, 23
Context
    developing students' understanding of, 37, 41, 44–47, 48, 59, 62, 65, 74, 82–84, 94, 103–122, 124, 126, 131–132
    expert knowledge and use of, 5, 9–10, 11, 14, 18, 19, 20, 30
    making connections with texts, 20, 38, 43, 56, 60, 75, 76, 81
    in scholarship of teaching and learning, 107, 109, 110, 127, 135
    in theories of reading, 14, 16
Course goals, 58–60, 70, 72–76, 80, 99–102
Course planning, xiv, xv, 36, 44, 58–59, 68, 69, 70–79, 80, 102
    matrix, 99–102
    process, 58–60, 70, 71, 72, 74, 79, 98–102
Courses
    American Novels, 65, 89
    American Popular Narratives, 45–47
    Immigrant Novels, 89

Introduction to Literary Study, 3, 26, 29, 40, 49

Senior Seminar, 59–60

Turn-of-the-Twentieth-Century American Literature, 34–35, 51, 53–57, 81–82

Working-Class Literature, ix, x

Critical debates, 22–23, 81, 90–91, 109–110, 133

Critical pedagogy, 3

Critical sources, ix, 13, 21, 24, 39, 45, 61, 83, 84, 89, 93

Cross-disciplinary collaboration, in scholarship of teaching and learning, 134–135

Culture of student learning, 141

Dialect, 18, 34–35, 38–39, 44

Difficulties
    in locating and using sources, 23, 44, 61–62, 82, 85, 115
    in reading, 1, 13, 14, 77, 113–114
    students', xi, 1, 4, 6, 27, 40, 48, 51, 96, 102, 105, 106, 108, 111, 112, 116, 117, 121–126, 127, 129, 137, 140, 147
    of texts, 13, 29, 34, 38, 39, 51, 113, 153n7

Discussion
    online, 51, 55, 68, 80, 89, 97, 114, 115, 116
    scaffolding of, 49–52, 53, 57, 62, 64–66, 67, 68, 80, 100
    and student learning, 14, 29, 30, 31, 33, 36, 39, 41–42, 43, 47, 59, 60, 74, 77–78, 125
    as a teaching method in English, ix–x, 3, 4, 29, 30, 35–36, 49, 87, 89, 95, 113

Dispositions, 8–14
    See also Habits of mind; Literary knowledge; Strategic knowledge

Donald, Janet Gail, 12, 21

Donohue, Patricia, 113, 153n7

Drafts, 57, 84, 91, 95

Dunbar, Paul Laurence, teaching of, 34–35, 38–39

Educational research, as resource for scholarship of teaching and learning, 112, 133

Educational Testing Service, 138

Enduring understandings, 72–76

English major
    goals for, xi–xiii, 2, 8, 23, 24–26, 36, 78, 86, 92
    requirements of, 26, 27–28
    value of, 2, 4, 25, 36–37, 73

English majors, 4, 6, 8, 11, 17, 25, 36, 48, 88, 127, 131, 139

Ethics, in scholarship of teaching and learning, 135–137

Evidence of student learning, 96, 105, 106, 107, 109, 116, 125, 136, 138, 143

Expert, as a model in learning, 38–39, 66, 71, 102

Expert reading, 14, 15–21, 24, 145

Expertise, xiv, 4, 5–7, 8, 11, 13, 21, 23, 27, 32, 43, 68, 69, 79, 93, 95, 98, 135
    adaptive, 5, 13, 18, 32, 37, 69
    as a hindrance to good teaching, 5–6, 8

Fading, 38, 78–79

Faerie Queen, The, teaching of, 77–79

Familiarity, as a course goal, 58–59, 75

Feminist pedagogy, x, 3

Focus groups, 127, 129, 151

Genre, as an element of literary study, ix, xi, 2, 8, 22, 25, 26, 27, 28, 57, 91

Grading, 48, 68, 85, 95–98, 116, 125

Habits of mind, xiv, 1, 2, 3, 6, 8, 11, 16–22, 32, 35, 44, 47, 48, 61, 66, 67, 84, 86, 87, 111, 120, 125, 142, 151
    See also Dispositions

Habitus, 6–7

House Behind the Cedars, The, teaching of, 53–55

How People Learn, 4, 33

Hypothesizing, 16, 20, 21, 41, 54, 57, 65, 86
    See also Provisional interpretations

Incremental learning, xv, 69, 79
    assignments for, 43, 72, 79, 87–88, 94
    See also Inquiry Project
Informal writing, 67, 68, 70, 80, 114, 115, 130
Inquiry project, 88–94, 96–97, 98, 116, 130
    See also Incremental learning
Institutional Review Board, 137, 150
Interdisciplinarity, 42–43, 127, 134, 147, 149
Interviews
    in scholarship of teaching and learning, 109, 110, 111, 113, 118, 126–129, 132, 136, 137, 151
    about teaching and learning in English, 74, 84, 153n5

Journals, in scholarship of teaching and learning, 133–134

Learning
    as a process, x, xiv, 6, 38, 71, 72, 78, 79, 90, 102
    theories and research about, xi, 2, 3, 4, 27, 33, 38, 43, 60, 71, 75, 79, 82, 99, 109, 133–135, 150 (*see also* Scholarship of Teaching and Learning)
    See also Cognitive Apprenticeship; Incremental learning; Interdisciplinarity
Learning-centered teaching, 72
Learning outcomes, in the English major, xi–xiii, 137–138
Learning to Think, 12
Lecture, as a teaching method, 29, 33, 35, 36, 39–40, 41, 42, 64, 65, 67, 68, 71, 80, 87
Literary analysis, 2, 3, 28, 42, 46, 52, 66, 68, 86, 87, 89, 126, 131

use in scholarship of teaching and learning, 107–109
    See also Context; Genre; Style; Themes
Literary argument, protocols for, 8, 21–24
Literary criticism, xii, 3, 10, 20, 23–24, 26, 31, 44, 82, 87, 90
    See also Critical sources; Literary theory
Literary knowledge, nature of, xiii, 2, 4–5, 43, 65, 67, 78, 87
    See also Content knowledge; Dispositions; Habits of mind; Strategic knowledge
Literary terms, xi, xiii, 2, 3, 18, 26, 58, 64
Literary theory, xiii, 2, 3, 4, 5, 8, 22, 25, 26, 31, 32, 42, 46, 74, 107, 133

McCormick, Kathleen, 14–15, 16, 20, 83
McTighe, Jay, 72–75, 102
Metacognition, 5, 13, 32, 54, 66, 68–69, 97, 126
Michael, Renee, 134
Mills, Andrew, 108–109
Modeling, 33, 38, 39–41, 43, 48, 49, 58, 60, 61, 65–67, 68, 69, 77–78, 83, 95
    examples of, 44–47, 52–57, 65
Modernism, 10, 49, 52
Multiculturalism, 3, 26

New criticism, 3, 10

"Pedagogy of the Distressed," 4
Poetry, 14, 34–35, 39–40, 77–78, 105, 112–113
Primary sources in literary study, 24, 45, 61, 63–64, 82, 83, 87, 90, 101, 109, 134
Problems, as starting point for scholarship of teaching and learning, 108–110, 111, 116, 133, 134, 142
Process-oriented teaching, 65, 72
Procrastination, 83–84, 92
Provisional interpretations, 15, 16, 20, 39, 86, 87
    See also Hypothesizing

Quantitative analysis, 107, 118, 138, 140
Questionnaires, 130–132, 145–149
Questions
    in class discussions, 30, 34, 41, 43,
        49, 55, 65, 66, 67, 95
    in course planning, 73, 75, 76, 77,
        79, 102
    as an element of literary research,
        12, 22, 23, 24, 32, 40, 45, 52, 53,
        54, 56, 57, 61, 65, 81, 85, 87–92,
        93, 118–119, 121
    as part of expert reading, 15–16,
        19, 20, 21
    in philosophy, 109
    in scholarship of teaching and
        learning, xiv, 105, 106, 107,
        108–109, 110, 111, 126–128,
        150–151
Quotes from critics, students' misuse of,
    61, 82, 84, 86, 90, 122–124

Reader-response theory, 3, 14, 132, 153n1
Reading, theories of, 14–17
Reading journal, 88–89, 93, 103, 114, 116,
    117–121, 124–126, 130
Reading literary criticism, 23–24, 90
Reflective writing, 88, 89, 92, 139
    prompts, 126, 132, 145–149
Rereading
    in literary analysis, 14, 20, 21, 86,
        88, 94
    in scholarship of teaching and
        learning, 116, 121, 125–126
Research paper, 29, 36, 79–87, 88, 91
    See also Inquiry Project
Responding to students' work, 57, 71, 80,
    86, 95–98, 115
    See also Coaching; Grading
Rosenblatt, Louise, 3
Rubrics, 48, 140

Salem, Anita, 134
Salvatori, Mariolina
    on difficulty, 113, 153n7
    on scholarship of teaching and
        learning, 107

Sample, selecting for research, 114–116,
    117, 121, 139–140
Sandefur, Jim, 112
Scaffolding, 39, 41–44, 47–52, 58, 60, 61,
    62, 68, 69, 79, 87–89, 95
    See also Incremental Learning,
        Inquiry project
Scholarly databases, 61, 83, 90, 134
Scholarly intuition, 22, 23
Scholarship of teaching and learning
    ethical considerations in, 135–137
    methods of, 111–132, 135
    value of, 107, 142–143
Scholes, Robert
    on the English major, 26, 31, 33,
        41, 98, 133
    on reading, 15–16, 19, 20
Secondary English, value of research on,
    132, 133, 134, 135
Showalter, Elaine
    on course goals, 25
    on course planning, 58, 70
    Teaching Literature, 25, 58, 70
    on teaching methods, 39–40
Shulman, Lee, 29, 30, 106
Signature pedagogy, 29–30, 36
Spark Notes, 14, 33
Strategic knowledge, xi, xiv, xv, 2–3, 54,
    66, 78, 81, 86, 98, 126, 142
    in course planning, 58–60, 70–72,
        74, 76, 99–101, 103–104
    of experts, 5–33
    scaffolding for, 43–47, 48, 52–53,
        87–88
    value of, 37–43
    See also Content knowledge;
        Dispositions; Habits of mind;
        Literary knowledge
Student independence, 39, 48, 77, 78,
    82, 98
Student portfolios, 92, 104, 139–140
Student work
    See Evidence of student learning
Students
    as novices, 4–5, 13, 18, 33, 38, 43,
        69, 71, 78, 150

perspectives on literature courses, 9, 32, 37, 64, 66, 74, 91, 126–132

reading habits, 1, 11, 13–14, 32, 55, 64, 77–78, 79–80, 83, 88, 107, 121

Style

literary, ix, 2, 3, 18, 74, 75, 76, 100, 103, 104, 132

strategies for teaching about, 48–52, 56, 117

students' analysis of, 1, 48–49, 51–52, 89, 93–94, 116, 118–120, 121–125, 132

Surveys

of English faculty, 10, 28, 29, 81, 131–132, 153n6

of English students, 117, 121, 126, 130, 131–132, 137, 145–149

Syllabi, 29, 65, 70, 102

Teaching anecdotes, 106–107

Text as construction, 11–12, 18

Textual analysis, 74, 89, 98, 131–132

Textual power, 98

Themes, as an element of literary study, xi, 38, 51, 56, 82, 89, 90, 93, 101, 105, 107, 113–114, 117, 123–124

Think aloud, 17, 52–54, 57, 66, 111–113, 114, 153n8

Tompkins, Jane, 4

Understanding, demonstration of, 70, 72, 73, 76–78, 79, 80–82, 87, 111, 114, 126, 128, 130, 131, 139, 151

Understanding by Design, 72

Videotaping, in scholarship of teaching and learning, 113, 114, 136, 149

Visible Knowledge Project, xv, 136

Webster, John, 77–79

Wiggins, Grant, 72–75, 102

Wineburg, Sam, 1–2, 8, 24, 33, 52, 111, 135

Working-class literature, ix, x, 4

Writing about literature, 26, 91

Writing assignments, as learning tools, 67–68, 70, 71, 80, 81, 86, 88

SHERRY LEE LINKON is a professor of English and American studies, and co-director of the Center for Working-Class Studies at Youngstown State University. She was a Carnegie Scholar in 1999, and in 2003 she was named Ohio Professor of the Year. She has edited several books, including *Teaching Working Class* (1999), and she is the co-author, with John Russo, of *Steeltown U.S.A.: Work and Memory in Youngstown* (2002). She has published articles and an online course portfolio about her research on teaching interdisciplinary analysis in literary and cultural studies, and she has given workshops and presentations on course design, interdisciplinary learning, teaching working-class students, and approaches to the scholarship of teaching and learning at colleges and universities around the country.